AMERICAN CHRISTIANITY

A Case Approach

Ronald C. White, Jr.
Louis B. Weeks
Garth M. Rosell

William B. Eerdmans Publishing Company
Grand Rapids, Michigan

Library of Congress Cataloging-in-Publication Data

American Christianity.

  Includes index.
  1. Christianity—United States—Case studies.
2. United States—Church history—Case studies.
I. White, Ronald C. (Ronald Cedric), 1939–
II. Weeks, Louis, 1941–   . III. Rosell, Garth.
BR515.A535   1986   277.3'092'6   86-16520

ISBN 0-8028-0241-3

Contents

List of Contributors

EDITORS

RONALD C. WHITE, JR., is director of continuing education and lecturer in church history at Princeton Theological Seminary. He is also the editor of *The Princeton Seminary Bulletin*. He has coauthored *The Social Gospel: Religion and Reform in Changing America* with C. Howard Hopkins. A forthcoming publication will be *The Dawn's Early Light: The Social Gospel and Racial Reform* (the Rauschenbusch Lectures).

LOUIS B. WEEKS is professor of historical theology at the Louisville Presbyterian Theological Seminary. He is also dean of the seminary. Among his recent publications are *Kentucky Presbyterians* and *To Be a Presbyterian*. He has edited several recent casebooks for Harper & Row, including *Full Value: Cases in Christian Business Ethics*, compiled by Oliver F. Williams and John W. Houck, and *Resolving Church Conflicts: A Case Study Approach for Local Congregations*, by G. Douglas Lewis. Weeks also coauthored *Casebook for Christian Living: Value Formation for Families and Congregations* (with Robert A. Evans et al.) and *Case Studies in Christ and Salvation* (with Jack Rogers and Ross Mackenzie).

GARTH M. ROSELL is vice president for academic affairs, dean of the seminary, and professor of church history at Gordon-Conwell Theological Seminary. He is currently serving as president of the Association for Case Teaching and has taught at both the Case Study Institute in Cambridge, Massachusetts, and the Case Method Institute in Pasadena, California. He is the author of *Cases in Theological Education* and is presently working with Richard A. G. Dupuis on a critical edition of the memoirs of Charles G. Finney.

OTHER CONTRIBUTORS

ROGER A. COUTURE is currrently on the staff of the Oblate Retreat House
in Hudson, New Hampshire, a Christian Renewal Center. Until recently professor of Christian and social ethics at Weston School of
Theology, he has published numerous case studies dealing with social, ecclesial, and ethical issues, among them (jointly with David
Brooks), "The National Council of Churches vs. Gulf & Western,"
appearing in *Full Value: Cases in Christian Business Ethics,* compiled
by Oliver F. Williams and John W. Houck (New York: Harper &
Row, 1978).

DONALD W. DAYTON is professor of theology and ethics at Northern
Baptist Theological Seminary. He has taught at Asbury Theological
Seminary and North Park Theological Seminary. He is a contributing
editor to *Sojourners,* having previously served as book editor. His
publications include *Discovering an Evangelical Heritage* and the
forthcoming *Theological Roots of Pentecostalism.*

PAUL T. DIEFFENBACH is supervisor of technical support services for the
St. Paul Fire and Marine Insurance Company. A graduate of the
University of Iowa and Bethel Theological Seminary, he has served as
a pastor in Rhode Island. He is an active participant in the ministry of
Woodbury Baptist Church in Woodbury, Minnesota.

SAMUEL GARRETT, now retired, taught church history at the Church
Divinity School of the Pacific and at the Graduate Theological Union,
Berkeley, California, from 1950 to 1984. His particular interests in-
clude British and American aspects of church history after 1500, and
he has written articles and reviews in those areas for *Church History,*
the *Anglican Theological Review,* and the *Historical Magazine of the
Episcopal Church.* He lives in Pacific Grove, near Monterrey,
California.

DONALD K. GORRELL is professor of church history at United Theological Seminary, Dayton, Ohio. He has edited *Woman's Rightful
Place* (1980) and has published articles in *Women in New Worlds*
(vol. 1, ed. Hilah F. Thomas and Rosemary S. Keller, Perspectives
on the Wesleyan Tradition Series [Nashville: Abingdon Press, 1981]),
Methodist History, the *Encyclopedia of World Biography,* and the
Encyclopedia of World Methodism. For twelve years he was secretary

of the General Commission on Archives and History of the United Methodist Church.

DOUGLAS H. GREGG is chaplain and associate professor of religious studies at Occidental College. He has written articles and case studies in American Christianity, Christian ethics, and college and young adult ministries. He is coauthor of *Case Studies in Higher Education Ministries* (1981).

DARREL M. ROBERTSON is author of several articles and review essays in the area of nineteenth-century revivalism. He has recently completed a book-length manuscript entitled *The Chicago Revival, 1876: A Study in the Sociology of Revival Religion.* He was formerly an assistant professor of history at the University of Iowa and presently serves as pastor of the Presbyterian-Congregational Church of Ashland, Wisconsin.

JACK ROGERS is professor of philosophical theology and associate provost for church relations at Fuller Theological Seminary. He has coauthored two books of historical case studies: *Case Studies in Christ and Salvation* (with Louis B. Weeks and Ross Mackenzie) and *Introduction to Philosophy: A Case Method Approach* (with Forrest Baird). His most recent publication is *Presbyterian Creeds: A Guide to the Book of Confessions.*

HENDRIKA VANDE KEMP is clinical psychologist and associate professor of psychology at Fuller Theological Seminary. She is the primary author of *Psychology and Theology in Western Thought, 1672-1965: A Historical and Annotated Bibliography.* She has also contributed historical articles to *The Journal of the History of the Behavioral Sciences, The American Psychologist, The Journal of Psychology and Theology,* and the *Baker Encyclopedia of Psychology.*

Acknowledgments

In preparing this volume for publication we are deeply conscious of many friends committed to increasing their effectiveness in teaching and learning. We express our thanks first of all to the Association for Case Teaching. Through its summer institutes we have learned a particular method employed in this book. Even more importantly we have been caught up in a style of education that fosters community rather than competition in learning. We are grateful to Alice Frazier Evans and Robert A. Evans, co-executive directors of ACT, for modeling what it means to teach and to learn. We acknowledge Marvin Taylor, who encouraged the case study method through his leadership with the Association of Theological Schools. We also want to thank Keith Bridston, who helped begin the Case Study Institute; M. B. (Jerry) Handspicker, who led several summer workshops; Jack Rogers, who has collaborated on a number of adaptations of cases for historical study; and Alan Neeley, who coordinates case writing for the Case Study Institute.

Many persons in different institutions have helped with the preparation and typing of these cases. We are limited to naming colleagues in our three institutions. Esther Flewelling, a member of the staff of Gordon-Conwell Theological Seminary, has worked for years with the preparation of cases for the ATS as well as working on this book. Norman Porterfield, Gloria Bryant, LaVerne Alexander, and Jean Knipp, all members of the Louisville Presbyterian Seminary staff, helped in the production of cases. Karen Wright, a member of the staff of the Center of Continuing Education at Princeton Theological Seminary, helped in the preparation of the index. And finally, a special thank you to Lynn S. Halverson, also of the Center of Continuing Education staff, who helped prepare the final manuscript for publication.

All of the cases in this book are also copyrighted by the Case Study Institute and are available for distribution through the Association for Theological Schools and the Association for Case Teaching.

Introduction

This volume is a presentation of major persons, ideas, issues, and movements in American Christianity by means of a case approach. These historical cases are designed primarily for classroom or group discussion. The book is designed to serve as a supplementary text in college and seminary courses, but we believe it can also be used with profit in churches to provide material for adult courses and leadership training. The cases can be used wherever students are seriously willing to study and discuss and wherever teachers are willing to prepare and enable them in the process.

LEARNING HISTORY THROUGH CASES

The chapters in this book are "case studies," written following patterns developed first at the Harvard Business School. A "case" is a description of an actual situation. It provides sufficient narrative and documentary data to enter vicariously into an historical situation. Usually the case is seen through the eyes of a person who must make an important decision. Often the case is left open-ended. Since the case is primarily a teaching tool, students are asked to study the situation and enter into an understanding of it as fully as they are able. They are to ask themselves, What would I have done?

Case studies of historical situations can enable us to understand the interests and intentions of significant leaders in our traditions. Then we can lay hold of the substance of their thought and bring it to bear on new situations that they could not have foreseen. Many of the case studies in this book are left deliberately unresolved. We often know or can easily discover the outcome, but our concern is not so much to tell the consequent history for discussion as it is to help the reader discover the process by which the resolution was attained. We want to understand the dynamic interaction of older precedents and new situations. Cases are designed to ask not just *what* happened but *why*.

HOW A CASE IS CONSTRUCTED

The cases in this book are generally constructed to follow the Harvard Business School "full text" method. With variations to suit the material, they tend to follow a four-point pattern. Part one gives the problem focus. Five items are generally contained in this opening section: the setting, the time, the decision maker, the specific decision to be made, and the larger issues involved. All of these are stated briefly and clearly. Thus the first paragraph or two should reveal what the case is about.

Part two is the historical context. It contains, usually in several paragraphs, the facts that the writer believes to be necessary as background for the case. The background provides a context for the narrative to follow. It tells what people need to know in general prior to dealing with the issues.

Part three is the narrative or exposition. This is usually the longest section. It traces the development of the problem in chronological sequence. We see the action from the perspective of one person, usually the decision maker in the case. We discover the attitudes of all who are involved as they relate to the decision maker. This narrative section culminates in a dramatic situation that poses the question to be decided.

Part four is a brief coda or reprise. Like the problem focus at the beginning, it encapsulates the setting, time, person, and issues. It brings the case to a conclusion by pointedly posing the questions that have to be discussed before a decision can be made.

Sometimes case studies add a fifth section of exhibits or appendices. Footnotes would disrupt the flow of involvement in the case and have been omitted in favor of a selective bibliography at the end of the case.

HOW THE STUDENT SHOULD PREPARE

Cases encourage cooperation rather than competition. After reading the case, students may wish to work in study groups. The discussion will reveal that each person has gleaned information and formed opinions not discovered by others. In addition to discussing the case, study groups could prepare written analyses of various aspects of the case. By dividing the responsibilities, all the students will benefit by having more data or diverse points of view or collateral documents presented. It is enormously rewarding when students discover that they can learn from one another. And it is humanizing to realize that it takes the combined efforts of many to do the best job. The group interaction in class reveals that many minds working together can clarify vistas and create viable solutions that are beyond what any single individual can do.

Study groups can be employed to present the initial discussion in class. Students can develop highly creative formats for introducing a case to the whole class: panel discussions, mini-plays, TV talk-show interviews, and visuals ranging from charts, graphs, and time lines to slides and films. Study groups can become case-writing groups as well. By dividing responsibilities and sharing resources, a group of five to seven students can research and write a significant case study during a quarter or a semester.

HOW THE CASE TEACHER SHOULD PREPARE

The case teacher will want to prepare a "teaching note" prior to the class discussion that includes several lists of data—an outline of the basic issues in the case, a time line to clarify the chronology of the case, and a cast of characters with brief biographical notes about each (including their relationships to one another). The teacher should also develop a tentative teaching plan incorporating several ideas of directions in which the case discussion could go. At times mini-lectures are effective in focusing historical material that students find "long ago and far away." Brief elucidation of particularly important and highly technical points may help to keep the discussion from getting bogged down.

The central function of the teacher in any case study situation is to serve as moderator and enabler. Ask penetrating questions. Write information on the blackboard. Be sure that all relevant information is before the group. Encourage students to interact in questioning and evaluating one another's views. The case teacher is a discussion leader. Willingness and ability to be flexible and follow the class is important. Various styles of discussion leadership will emerge, suiting the case content and the teacher's personality.

A wide variety of case leadership styles are effective. The needs of the group and the authenticity of the teacher/student relationship count for more than any one way of leading the class. Some people seem more at home with patterned, forceful direction. Others function best in comparative freedom. Discerning the appropriate style (i.e., a comfortable and helpful style) takes experience and sensitivity, not adherence to formulaic rules.

An ideal class period lasts from about ninety minutes to two hours. The first half of the period can be used to clarify the data, with the teacher asking questions and writing student responses on the chalkboard. The second half of the period can be devoted to analyzing the issues in the case and advocating and debating various points of view.

APPROPRIATING HISTORY THROUGH CASES

These case studies are intended to be as objective as possible. Their open-ended style encourages the reader to resist hasty judgments. The cases in this book make no attempt to present all interpretations of events current among competent historians. Generally, writers have followed prevailing schools of thought rather than introducing perspectives that are extreme. One significant difference from most textbooks, however, is the strict chronological ordering of events in the cases. Most historians order such events in keeping with certain interpretative interests, but the case study method depends on the readers being able to follow the events with the principal decision maker. With the original time sequence as the organizing principle, the reader has the opportunity to enter vicariously into the experience and do his or her own interpreting. No hypothetical situations are created. No disguises are used. The actual facts are presented as well as the writers could reconstruct them in brief compass. Normal literary license is occasionally used to create dialogue and to attribute feelings to characters, but in all such cases the writers have been careful to attribute to the characters only what seem demonstrably to have been their actual attitudes.

Historical case studies can be useful for anyone who wants to deal with significant issues in their original environment. Many of the cases in this book have already been widely used in college and seminary classrooms, in doctor of ministry courses and in continuing education seminars for pastors. Lay people taking seminary extension courses have found them an appealing alternative to traditional approaches to church history. Youth workers have discovered in them both a content and a technique that they could profitably apply. All manner of people have discovered in case studies a way to read historical theology that offers the content of a textbook but the fascinating form of a detective story or drama. Case studies are not equally valuable in all learning contexts, but they do offer tantalizing possibilities in a vast number of situations.

As you use these cases, we would appreciate your sharing the results with us. In this time of pioneering in the use of inductive teaching methods, we are hoping to find further means of teaching and learning that will enrich the spiritual resources, ethical sensibilities, and sheer knowledge of us all. Too often as educators we have settled for giving students predigested results, thereby depriving them of the excitement of discovery that has motivated us. Our purpose in this book is to provide materials relating to the study of American religious history that will allow each person to make his or her own evaluation. It is because of the enjoyment, involvement, and understanding we have received in working with historical cases that we are pleased to present this collection for your use.

Ronald C. White, Jr.
Louis B. Weeks
Garth M. Rosell

AMERICAN CHRISTIANITY

Part One

Origins

American Christianity grew from European churches, at least in its beginning. Spanish and French Catholics, Anglicans, Dutch Reformed, German Lutherans, Scot Presbyterians, and others from areas in which official church relations with state held sway at first took it for granted that their religion would extend organizationally to the New World. Christopher Columbus simply assumed that Spain owned the whole of the Western hemisphere. He thought Spanish Catholics would Christianize it both by colonizing it and by sending missionaries to convert the "heathen" already there. Explorers and settlers with allegiance to England or France sometimes grew less ambitious as they learned more of the situation, but they retained the general worldview of "extension"— that New England or New France would recapitulate in religious matters the very best of their memory and hope concerning what the "Old" countries were (or should have been).

Decisions to establish dioceses of San Domingo, Concepçion, and San Juan as suffragen sees of Seville in Spain seemed perfectly natural. The same mentality permitted the Bishop of London oversight of British colonies in the West. Much of the origin of American Christianity, then, grew from implicit assumptions that the new would simply extend what already existed. Parochialism, popular piety, and contentiousness had characterized European churches, and these sentiments crossed the Atlantic very quickly (if indeed they were not already present among native Americans in forms other than the European Christian expressions).

American Christianity was born parochial. With a few exceptions, the religious among the colonists left little room for active disagreement within their first communing groups. Catholics in New France sometimes gave Huguenots a hard time. Dutch Reformed Christians under Peter Stuyvesant jailed Lutherans. Puritans persecuted Quakers, executed four Anglicans, and incarcerated and fined both Baptists and Presbyterians.

1

On the other hand, worshiping and working groups in some of the more settled areas did remain close-knit and cared deeply for one another. Thus both the positive and negative aspects of parochialism were present—constituting exile for dissidents but also providing parish-type support for neighbors in all realms of life.

Popular piety, too, was evident from the beginning. Gabriel Diza Vara Calderon, Bishop of Cuba, reported with pride that Christianized Indians not only went regularly to mass in Florida in 1674 but also took turns praying the rosary during Holy Week in groups of twenty-four men, twenty-four women, twenty-four boys, and twenty-four girls—rotating groups hourly, as was the fashion of prayer in Spain at that time. The witchcraft episodes in Salem, as elsewhere, were symptoms of the power of popular piety according to many scholars of colonial American historians. Dale's Laws in Virginia required that "everie man and woman duly twice a day upon the first towling of the Bell shall upon the working dais repaire unto the Church, to hear divine Service." Those who missed once would lose the day's wages; those who missed twice would be whipped; those who missed thrice stood condemned "to the Gallies for six Moneths."

Contentiousness likewise came as a component of Christianity. French Catholics resented the fact that Spanish Catholics controlled some religious orders, and vice versa. New Englanders scowled at the demise of Puritanism further south when control of the Virginia Company changed hands in 1624. The Puritan leaders frowned on internal dissent and private interpretation as in the case of Anne Hutchinson. Lutherans feared "loss of faith" in New Amsterdam because Reformed Dutch were in command.

But if immigrant religious baggage included some sentiments of an ambiguous if not outright negative nature, it also included hope. Many of those coming to America were dedicated to the ideal of advancing the kingdom of God, even though their methods eventuated more in the advance of national and parochial Christianity. At least they were inspired by the possibilities and the idea of advancing. To Puritan spirits, their journey represented an "errand into the wilderness" on behalf of a new Israel. John Winthrop tempered promise with warning but suggested that the new community in 1630 could be "as a Citty upon a Hill" if the people remained faithful. Eighteen years earlier, Pierre Biard, a Jesuit missionary in New France, had written that Indians in Port Royal "received the first faint ideas and seeds of our holy faith, which will germinate abundantly, if God is willing, some day, and if there is better cultivation."

All of the people came with hopes—although the hopes of the Christians sometimes conflicted. Biard, in the course of his narrative, reports his delight at having helped to "dispatch" some British interlopers. Winthrop bemoans the "Papists." But, with some notable exceptions, colonial America afforded believers enough room to celebrate their diverse aspirations. Roman Catholics may have found little to warm the heart in Plymouth, but they were usually tolerated and even supported in Maryland. Scot-Irish Presbyterians discovered they could leap-frog the seaboard and cluster in the valleys of Virginia and Pennsylvania and the semihighland areas of North Carolina. Baptists persecuted in Virginia were at home in Rhode Island. Quakers, after they toned down a bit, found midland homesteads in Pennsylvania and the Jerseys. Dutch Reformed settled comfortably in New York, née New Amsterdam. Further north and west, colonies of France and Spain existed, and some thrived. Colonial confrontations appear to have been provoked chiefly by European initiation—not social or religious hostility in the colonies themselves.

There were similarities in the sentiments of the colonists to be sure, but there were likewise vast differences in their experience and situations. Some came as "gentlemen," others as "yeomen." Historian Mary Beard long ago pointed out that some women journeying to the colonies may have owned property like the men, but they saw the wilderness from a different perspective. Indentured servants certainly possessed different expressions of hope from the newly emergent professionals. Those young people sold or given by European parents to traders who brought them to work for or to wife the colonists already able to pay for them no doubt viewed all of life quite differently than those who chose to "seek their fortunes" on new shores. And imagine the differences between the perspective of European Christian immigrants and the African victims of mass kidnappings, degraded as slaves and "Christianized."

The mélange of peoples, with conflicting ethnic identities and class or even caste affiliations, made colonial American religion as distinctive as other aspects of colonial American life. Among Presbyterians, for example, English Puritans of connectional ecclesiology may have affirmed the Westminster Standards their progenitors wrote, but they emphasized the primacy of biblical authority over any creedal statement. And they believed strongly that the essence of Christianity lay in living a pious life. Scots, Presbyterians, and those who came to be termed Scotch-Irish viewed subscription to the Westminster Confession and catechisms as part and parcel of the Christian worldview. The deep split that colonial

Presbyterianism endured had already healed by the time of the American Revolution. A new Presbyterianism developed in the novel environment, characterized among other things by diminished solidarity of Scotch-Irish communities and a reduction in the piety of their confessionalism. Likewise, Puritanism of the connectional variety lost some of its holistic fervor for holy life in terms of both the individual and the world. But the resultant denomination went beyond ethnic compromise to form an American tradition. It offered Presbyterians a religious dynamism that fostered the beginnings of American revivalism and in time began to feed European parent churches as well.

Necessity led Anglicans in America to develop a system of vestry, providing a responsible role for lay people. Methodism flourished in the colonies as a pietist movement, and Baptists experimented with Calvinism and Arminianism, with "gospel discipline" and religious freedom. Congregationalists early developed a cultural Protestantism that offered harmony with other Christian communions, although some of them sought to reinstill the force of piety in the churches that they felt had been tragically lost in the demise of Puritan theocracy.

Quakers, with early access to American colonies, held a special place in the synthesis of American Christianity. They truly sought to provide freedom of worship for all. In North Carolina, South Carolina, Virginia, and the Jerseys, in New Amsterdam and Rhode Island, and ultimately in Pennsylvania, the Quakers prospered—despite occasional harassment. Disciples of the "Inner Light" introduced the possibility (threat?) of living amicably in a spiritual democracy in which young and old, men and women all received divine inspiration. Their pacifism shook the foundation of the "church militant" in its various expressions Catholic and Protestant. And their prophecy, as in the case of John Woolman, worked to undo the structure of the developing institution of slavery.

Slavery existed in the northern colonies, but its impact was felt primarily in the southern ones. Recent scholarship suggests that evangelical Christianity as we know it grew from the enfranchisement of the Southern poor at the expense of traditional authority patterns as well as from the amalgam of African animistic religion with the Christian worldview as black people forged it. No competent scholar questions the importance of black Afro-American Christians in the development of American Christianity. In their slavery, seeking their freedom, they opened the hermeneutics of liberation that Christianity offered; it would appear that few colonial whites employing images of the promised land, the new birth, or freedom itself thought through their implications for black America.

The participation of native Americans in the origins of American

Christianity constitutes another poignant story. Newcomers found native Americans both enemies and friends, hosts and trespassers, savages and masters from whom to learn in apprenticeship. The ambiguities of relationship between the colonists and the indigenous peoples persist even today. Spaniards began missionary activity almost immediately—possibly as early as 1521. Dominicans, Franciscans, and Jesuits especially introduced Christianity across the "sunbelt." Franciscans worked in New Mexico, Florida, and in between throughout the seventeenth century, converting thousands before the time of the coming of "settlers." In 1784 Father Junipero Serra estimated that he had confirmed 5,307 native American Christians in California missions such as San Diego, Monterrey, and San Francisco. French Jesuit missionaries labored from the St. Lawrence corridor to the Gulf of Mexico, and more thousands professed Christianity as a result of their efforts. Puritans and Quakers in particular sent missionaries to tribes living near English colonies, and more thousands claimed Christian commitment. Native Americans were clearly a significant target of colonial American religious missions.

On the other hand, with few exceptions the native Americans were offered little opportunity to contribute their own insights in the fashioning of American Christianity. They got even less of a chance to synthesize the new faith with their own previous religious experiences. They appeared as "Canaanites" to an arriving "Israel," to be destroyed according to God's purposes. Most often, colonial Americans treated them as objects—tools for a fur trade or a mining enterprise, keys to easily taken land and food, or even as spiritual trophies to call for additional missionary support.

The English colonies in America, most determinative for later American Christianity, grew fiercely, and the numbers of churches expanded as quickly. One major factor in this expansion was certainly the migration of European pietists to America. Another was the "Great Awakening" that rocked the colonial religious establishment thoroughly during the 1740s, fed by the preaching of Jonathan Edwards, George Whitefield, and a host of other ministers.

Edwin Gaustad estimates that in 1780 there were 749 Congregational churches, 495 Presbyterian, 457 Baptist, 406 Anglican, 240 Lutheran, 228 Reformed (Dutch and German), and 56 Catholic. Some of these communities were quite small; others possessed hundreds of members. The allegiances of colonists at the time of the American Revolution probably coincided in rough proportion to the numbers of parishes and congregations. Some colonists claimed no Christian identification at all; a few professed Judaism. It is likely that a great many—perhaps most—

of the colonists associated themselves with one or another of the Christian denominations on the basis of ethnic ties or vaguely related belief systems without exercising any deeper connection in daily life.

Denominational mobility had already begun for some in colonial America. Anglican vestryman Robert Carter III joined a Virginia Baptist congregation in 1778. (He converted to Swedenborgianism before his death.) Judith Sargent, the Massachusetts author, announced her affection for Universalism and as a widow married the itinerant preacher John Murray, who founded the first Universalist meeting house in America in 1780. Numbers of Puritans moved to Quakerism; and George Keith, the Quaker leader in a colonial schism, began and wound up an Anglican. The quality of Keithian Quakers, a "finer sort" according to Puritan divine Cotton Mather, prompted many to reassess their anathema on Christian communions that they had once considered ungodly. Among those colonial Christians who were changing allegiances and also those who had identified with denominations as a result of conversion experiences rather than long-term nurture in the church, there began to arise questions about the limits of authority and the efficacy of the established order.

The mention of Universalism and Swedenborgianism prompts a reminder that more *outre* expressions of Christianity found their way to America by the close of the eighteenth century. Moravians came, and so did numbers of Continental Anabaptist groups. "Seventh-day men," believers in Sabbatarian Christianity, had long been active, though many Bible readers similarly critical of mainstream religion were anti-Sabbatarian. Unitarian and Deistic beliefs were entertained by some, cherished by others. Shakers arrived in 1776, but Shakerism rose in popularity only later.

The English colonies remained under the threat of violence if not under actual attack throughout most of the colonial period. In early years, "wars and rumors of wars" were largely a matter of Indian attacks. Sometimes in concert with European conflicts (as the Thirty Years' War, 1618-48), frequently egged on by colonial incursions, Indians made severe attacks on settlements. Jamestown, in Virginia, lost almost a third of its people in 1622. Early on, Pequot killed some colonists in the Connecticut River valley. Needless to say, settlers' militia usually "retaliated" by murdering hundreds of members of various tribes, as in the Jamestown and Connecticut River incidents. Later wars became more rapacious. In the Deerfield massacre (1704), Indians and French-Canadians not only killed about forty residents of the village in a surprise attack but marched more than a hundred back to Montreal—three hundred miles away—as prisoners. Massachusetts took Indian prisoners in return, killing a number in the process. In King George's War and in the Seven Years' War, colonists from several English regions fought colonists from New France, with native Americans allies on both sides. Militarism was virtually a permanent fixture of colonial life.

The threat of hostilities has been cited as one of the possible causes of the Great Awakening, which imprinted American Christianity as a distinctive enterprise in the 1740s. The revival movement provoked serious opposition of the "disorders" that frequently accompanied conversions. But Jonathan Edwards, the most noted of the Great Awakening divines, adhered to many traditional values in theology and considered the conversions "surprising." Subsequently, the Great Awakening has been viewed as a unifying force among American Christians, a movement helping mold a new identity for a people.

By the same token, American Christianity grew as colonists sought to achieve cultures of their own. Granted, their ideas of civilization were patterned upon the European. Puritans objected to some of the facets of Old World life—theater, the singing of light songs, the opulence of drawing rooms, and so on. But on the whole they approved of the study of science and the regularization of living habits in an etiquette. Other colonists without religious scruples against fun simply could not capture all the nuances of high society with their limited resources. They did manage to hire tutors as quickly as possible when they could afford them, to construct schools when enough people would cooperate to do so, and to establish other institutions essential to the formation of larger communities—banks, depots, taverns, and commons (not necessarily in that order).

Institutions of higher education—William and Mary in Virginia, Harvard in Massachusetts, Yale in Connecticut, Brown in Rhode Island, and log colleges all over the colonies modeled on the one at Princeton—profoundly affected the course of American religion as leaders emerged from them to shape the future. Whether by fostering liberal ideas or just by offering regular courses of study for ministers-to-be, the colonial colleges taught Americans to conjoin learning from Europe with experiences from the New World.

The Revolution, though opposed by many American Christians and ignored by others, gave promise to most Protestant leaders of new order, of a nation in which the faithful could work and worship with religious freedom. Isaac Backus and the Baptists hoped for such freedom, as did many Presbyterians and Congregationalists. Those in the gathered communions that had formerly been persecuted raised especially fervent prayers for space and rights unfettered by the state.

SELECTED BIBLIOGRAPHY

Beard, Mary. *America through Women's Eyes.* New York: Macmillan, 1933.

Blau, Joseph, and Salo Baron. *The Jews of the United States.* 3 vols. New York: Columbia University Press, 1963.

Bucke, Emory S. *The History of American Methodism.* Vol. 1. Nashville: Abingdon Press, 1964.

Gaustad, Edwin. *Historical Atlas of Religion in American Life.* New York: Harper & Row, 1962.

————. *Religious Issues in American History.* New York: Harper & Row, 1968. Chapters 1-4.

Matthews, Donald G. *Religion in the Old South.* Chicago: University of Chicago Press, 1977.

Peckham, Howard H. *The Colonial Wars, 1689-1762.* Chicago: University of Chicago Press, 1964.

Shea, John G. *History of the Catholic Missions among the Indian Tribes of the United States.* New York: Edward Dunigan, 1855.

Thwaites, Ruben, ed. *The Jesuit Relations and Allied Documents.* New York: Pageant Book, 1959.

Trinterud, Leonard. *The Forming of an American Tradition.* Select Bibliographies Reprint Series. Salem, N.H.: Ayer, 1949.

Wertenbaker, Thomas J. *The Founding of American Civilization.* 3 vols. New York: Scribner's, 1938-47.

Wise, Winifred. *Fray Junipero Serra and the California Conquest.* New York: Scribner's, 1967.

Anne Hutchinson and the Puritans of Massachusetts Bay Colony

This case was prepared by Garth M. Rosell

"Mrs. Hutchinson," Governor John Winthrop declared following the divided vote, it is the decision of the General Court of the Massachusetts Bay Colony that you are to be "banished from out of our jurisdiction as being a woman not fit for our society, and are to be imprisoned till the court shall send you away." Anne Hutchinson sat quietly as Winthrop spoke. Through her mind passed many of the remarkable events that had brought her to this difficult moment.

ANNE HUTCHINSON

Born in 1591, the second of Bridget and Francis Marbury's thirteen children, Anne spent her early years in Alford, Lincolnshire, a village in the North Midlands of England. Her father, an Anglican minister, was an outspoken critic of all forms of established authority, including the church. An independent spirit, he frequently called his ministerial colleagues to account for what he felt was their lack of training and ability. Such activity outraged many in the church. Shortly before Anne's birth, his superiors deprived him of all ministerial support.

At the age of twenty-one, on 9 August 1612, Anne married William Hutchinson, son of an Alford textile merchant. The young couple and their expanding family (fifteen children—six boys and nine girls—were born to the Hutchinsons between 1613 and 1636) soon began attending worship at St. Botolph's in Boston, a city some twenty miles south of Alford. What drew them to the church was the preaching of the Reverend Mr. John Cotton, who in 1612 had left his job as tutor in Emmanuel College, Cambridge, to become vicar of the Boston parish.

JOHN COTTON

Cotton's preaching was clearly Puritan in form and content, combining a sense of dissatisfaction with the insufficiently Reformed nature of the Church of England and an emphasis on experiential faith. Unlike many of his Puritan colleagues, however, Cotton tended to stress what he called the covenant of grace rather than the covenant of works. Sanctification, Cotton had come to believe, should not be seen as a primary evidence of God's election to salvation. While God expects his children to live holy lives, a person's upright moral conduct should not be taken as proof of God's redemptive grace. Assurance of salvation, insofar as it can be achieved, must rest primarily upon the inward witness of the Holy Spirit.

Cotton's Puritan leanings brought him increasingly into conflict with his Anglican superiors. By 1633, the tensions had increased to the point that Cotton was forced to flee his parish and homeland to avoid imprisonment for nonconformity. Setting sail for America at the age of forty-eight, Cotton arrived in the Bay Colony a few months later, was welcomed warmly by the settlers there, and was installed as pastor of the Boston church.

PURITANISM IN THE MASSACHUSETTS BAY COLONY

Cotton was pleased with what he found in the New World. Established only three years before, the Massachusetts Bay Colony was thoroughly Puritan in design. Possessed of a profound sense of destiny, its early leaders hoped that Boston would become a "city upon a hill." Believing that God had chosen them as his "new Israel," the Bay Colony leaders set themselves to the task of building a truly Christian society, founded on the teachings of the Bible (as interpreted by the reverend elders) and unified around a common mission. Far from advocating religious liberty, these early Puritans expected the whole community to believe and behave alike. Yearning to reform the Church of England by example, these nonseparating Puritans felt that simply too much was at stake to allow for religious diversity within the colony.

While the Bay Colony leaders were glad to welcome Cotton into their midst, many of his parishioners in England were devastated by his departure. Among those most profoundly troubled was Anne Hutchinson. Informed by what she believed to be a divine revelation to follow her pastor to America, Anne and her family set sail for Massachusetts Bay in May. By September of 1634 the ship had anchored in Boston harbor.

The Hutchinsons found their places quickly at the top level of colonial society. William, whose cloth business was soon thriving, was voted a Boston selectman and deputy to the General Court. Anne set herself to the task of raising a family, serving as a midwife, and helping to nurse the sick in the community.

Soon also the Hutchinsons were opening their home to members of the Boston church, men and women alike, who wished to come to hear Anne's restatement of the previous Sunday's sermon. Increasingly, members of the congregation came to rely upon Anne to explain the difficult theological meanings of their pastor's tightly reasoned sermons. Among those who attended were many of Boston's most prominent citizens, including the colony's governor, Henry Vane, and most of the town's leading merchants.

CONFLICT IN THE COMMUNITY

As the months passed, however, Anne, who had become increasingly disturbed by what she felt was the community's undue emphasis upon sanctification as a primary evidence of election, began to expound her own distinctive understanding of Puritan theology. Having discovered the covenant of grace through the preaching of Cotton, she was soon pressing the matter in far more extreme forms than had her pastor. Anne believed that the elect, indwelled by the Holy Spirit, were released from the moral law of the Old Testament by the advent of a new dispensation of grace introduced by the coming of Christ. One's moral conduct, she had come to believe, was of no essential value in validating one's election or in providing assurance of one's salvation. Such assurance comes only through the inner witness of the Spirit. It flows from grace rather than works.

Anne's teaching soon produced a sharp division within the community. This polarity was further exacerbated when the Reverend Mr. John Wilson, having returned in 1635 from a trip to England, began to share preaching responsibilities with Cotton in the Boston pulpit. Disturbed by what she felt was Wilson's emphasis on the covenant of works, Anne suggested that he (along with most of the Bay Colony clergy) lacked the "seal of the Spirit." In Anne's eyes, only John Cotton and the Reverend Mr. John Wheelwright (her brother-in-law) were preaching the true faith.

Tensions between the two factions increased through 1636. By January of 1637 the situation had come to a head. Having set aside January 19 as a day of general fasting and prayer for God's healing of the "dissensions in our church," the Bay Colony leaders had invited John Wheelwright to preach the fast day sermon in the Boston church. The strategy produced anything but healing. Indeed, Wheelwright's sermon—which clearly reflected the leanings of the Hutchinson faction—produced a violent reaction within the community.

TRIAL

By March, the General Court (itself divided) had found it necessary to bring Wheelwright to trial. After deliberation, it found him guilty of "contempt" and "sedition." The Court's action did not go unnoticed. A "remonstrance" protesting Wheelwright's conviction was circulated among the members of the Boston church (sixty signatures were collected) and then presented to the General Court.

As might be expected under these circumstances, the May elections in the colony were hotly contested. Drawing its strength largely from outlying areas, the traditionalist faction succeeded in electing one of its own, John Winthrop, as governor and in ousting several members of the Hutchinson faction from the General Court. By September the traditionalist forces had clearly consolidated their strength in the churches as well. At a meeting of synod that month, the Bay Colony churches officially condemned Anne Hutchinson's teachings as both dangerous and untrue.

It remained only for the General Court, at a November session, to conclude the matter. John Wheelwright, having been earlier condemned for sedition and contempt, was banished from the colony. Others likewise were either disfranchised or banished for having signed the remonstrance. Anne Hutchinson, for her part, was brought to trial for "traducing the ministers and their ministry."

"Mrs. Hutchinson," Governor John Winthrop declared following the divided vote, it is the decision of the General Court of the Massachusetts Bay Colony that you are to be "banished from out of our jurisdiction as being a woman not fit for our society, and are to be imprisoned till the court shall send you away." By March of 1638, she and her family were gone.

SELECTED BIBLIOGRAPHY

Adams, Charles Francis, ed. *Antinomianism in the Colony of Massachusetts Bay, 1636-1638*. Boston: The Prince Society, 1894.

Battis, Emery. *Saints and Sectaries: Anne Hutchinson and the Antinomian Controversy in the Massachusetts Bay Colony*. Chapel Hill, N.C.: University of North Carolina Press, 1962.

Hall, David D., ed. *The Antinomian Controversy, 1636-1638: A Documentary History*. Middletown, Conn.: Wesleyan University Press, 1968.

Morgan, Edmund S. "The Case Against Anne Hutchinson." *New England Quarterly*, December 1937.

Rugg, Winifred King. *Unafraid: A Life of Anne Hutchinson*. Boston: Houghton Mifflin, 1930.

Rushing, Jane Gilmore. *Covenant of Grace: A Novel of Anne Hutchinson*. Garden City, N.Y.: Doubleday, 1982.

Stoever, William K. B. *"A Faire and Easie Way to Heaven": Covenant Theology and Antinomianism in Early Massachusetts*. Middletown, Conn.: Wesleyan University Press, 1978.

Cotton Mather and the Salem Witch Trials

This case was prepared by Hendrika Vande Kemp

NOTE: This case, more than most others, demands that the reader participate, insofar as possible, in a worldview shared by most at the turn
of the eighteenth century. A key aspect of this worldview was the
belief that angels and evil spirits are indeed messengers from God
and the devil, bearing intermediate power and subject only to divine authorities. Cotton Mather, the people of Salem, scientists
Joseph Glanville and Robert Boyle, and most others considered this
worldview to have been validly derived from the Bible, from evidences in their lives, and from religious tradition.

Cotton Mather, Puritan divine, felt too ill to make the trip himself in
the spring of 1692, but he wanted to share his wisdom with the people of
Salem, their magistrates, and the judges sent to hear the cases of witchcraft. He had experienced the effects of such supernatural activities, and
he wanted others to benefit from his learning. Most of all, though, he
wanted Christians to be faithful in their living. He struggled to write John
Richards, who would be a judge in the matter. He found it extremely
difficult to state his position.

COTTON MATHER

Born in February 1663, the son of Increase and Maria Mather, the boy
was named Cotton in honor of her father, John Cotton, a Puritan divine
like Increase Mather. Frequently ill as an infant, Cotton Mather received
very special treatment from his parents and the finest education available
in Boston, the center of intellectual life in the Massachusetts colony. In
1669, Richard Mather, father of Increase and also a Puritan religious
leader, died; grandson Cotton saw his father almost die that fall as well.
Home studies for Cotton Mather were mixed with formal instruction at

the Boston Latin School and Harvard College, where he received both the bachelor's and master's degrees offered there. In 1685, he joined his father as a minister of Boston's Second Church, a pastorate he would hold until 1723. He married Abigail Phillips, of Charlestown, in 1686.

Mather maintained from childhood an intense interest in sciences of all sorts. He studied medicine in his youth and later developed interests in astronomy, physics, and especially biology.

Mather used his scientific training and his theology in ministering to the children of John Goodwin and his wife, especially to Martha Goodwin, whom the Mathers took into their home in 1688. A year later Mather published a study entitled *Memorable Providences Relating to Witchcrafts and Possessions,* which was a record of the gradual improvement under family care of the Goodwin girl, who exhibited possession by demons. The work tells how Martha could be quietly studying Scripture in Mather's library and then be violently seized when she went back downstairs. Mainly, Mather believed Martha to have been healed by fervent and persistent prayer.

Altogether, the girl spent about six weeks in the Mather home, and several months later she joined Second Church. In 1691 and 1692 Mather published two other works on witchcraft. Thus, he developed a reputation for knowledge and experience in successfully coping with apparent demon posession that would be considered valuable as events in Salem began to unfold.

SALEM: SETTLEMENT AND LEADERS

The town of Salem began in 1626, when Roger Conant selected it as a likely spot to found a fishing station and trading post. Salem soon outgrew its original site, where the soil proved insufficiently fertile to provide food for the growing population in the 1630s. In 1639 the General Court began to permit settlement inland, and Salem Town leaders made land grants in what became known as Salem Village. Town government extended to encompass the Village as well, though the farming populace of the Village felt it was being discriminated against by the trading populace of the Town.

Initially, the clergy of Salem Town served Salem Village as well. When a separate minister was called, General Court specified all householders should participate, for there were not yet sufficient church members to form a self-sustaining body. In 1672, the men of Salem Village elected James Bayley of Newbury as preacher. Bayley began to serve the

Village, but dissidents acted the next year to withhold payments on his salary. After several years of acrimony between critics and proponents of Bayley, the minister finally gave up the fight and left Salem Village in 1680. His replacement, George Burroughs, came from the Casco Bay settlement after it had been decimated by an Indian attack. He did not fare much better than Bayley and left in 1683 to resume work at Casco Bay, again in arrears in salary payments and owing several creditors.

The Reverend Deodat Lawson served Salem Village from 1684 to 1688. Then the Reverend Samuel Parris served from 1688 until the witchcraft episodes began. Both these ministers were similarly implicated in the conflict between Town and Village. Lawson was denied installation in the process, and Parris was subjected to the party strife that by 1688 had become a veritable tradition.

THE WITCHCRAFT EPISODES

The daughter and niece of Samuel Parris first experienced sickness in the winter of 1692. Physicians could not help them; one of them speculated that witchcraft might be to blame.

Other young girls began to report the same symptoms—pains as though they were being stuck with pins or irons. One of these girls identified three women—"Gammer" Osborne, a bed-ridden invalid; Tituba, the slave of Parris; and Sarah Good, a Village pauper—as the culprits. Examinations in Salem Village produced no confessions, but "spectral evidence" was admitted: the girls were able to accuse the women in person, and the girls' violent actions in court were taken as proof of the women's guilt.

Examination of these three women continued on the third and fifth of March, and on the seventh day they were sent to Boston jail, where they were gradually joined by other accused witches. On April 11 the hearings were moved from Salem Village to Salem Town. Jonathan Corwin and John Hawthorne were joined as judges by four other magistrates, including Samuel Sewall (whose diary provides detailed personal records of the events) and Thomas Danforth, the deputy-governor of the colony, who acted as presiding magistrate. Apparently, proceedings did not change much at this time. Hawthorne began by asking John Indian, who had joined the ranks of the afflicted, who had hurt him. Elizabeth Procter and Sarah Cloyce were then accused not only of choking him but also of bringing him the Devil's book to sign. He was asked if he knew these women personally, or only their apparitions. Upon claiming acquaintance with Goody Cloyce, she burst out at him, "When did I hurt thee?"

and he answered, "A great many times." Further evidence was brought against Goodwife Cloyce by Abigail Williams and Mary Walcott, who claimed they had seen her at a meeting of witches at Deacon Ingersoll's.

During the month of May, accusations of witchcraft expanded at an alarming rate, an increasing number finding themselves in jail. Local officials impatiently waited for action by Colony officials, which came on May 27: the governor's council set up a General Court which immediately appointed a Special Court of Oyer and Terminer. Such courts were established on a temporary basis to deal with unusual cases or to hear temporary allegations that developed while permanent courts were adjourned. Their authorizing commissions dissolved as soon as the specific trial for which they were convened was over. Governor Phips appointed as his chief justice Lieutenant Governor William Stoughton of Dorchester. From Boston he selected Samuel Sewall, Wait Winthrop, John Richard, and William (or Peter) Sergeant. Nathaniel Saltonstall was summoned from Haverhill, and Bartholomew Gedney from Salem. Captain Stephen Sewall served as clerk of the court, and Thomas Newton as King's attorney.

Faced with a situation in which the truth was difficult to find, at least one of the justices sought expert advice: John Richards wrote to the Reverend Cotton Mather, asking him to be present at the first trial.

MATHER'S QUANDARY

William Phips, the newly appointed governor of Massachusetts, appointed the tribunal as one of his first official acts. A special friend of Cotton Mather, Phips arrived in the colony after several accused witches were in jail. Mather, wanting desperately to help secure the position of Phips in the government, had as an overriding aim the maintenance of Puritan control.

At the same time, he recognized the need to combat the wiles of Satan. It would be cowardly and unfaithful behavior not to confront evil spirits and overcome them in behalf of Christian peace and justice.

Mather contemplated advice for Richards and the other judges.

SELECTED BIBLIOGRAPHY

Booth, Sally Smith. *The Witches of Early America*. New York: Hastings House, 1975.

Boyer, Paul, and Stephen Nissenbaum. *Salem Possessed: The Social Origins of Witchcraft.* Cambridge: Harvard University Press, 1974.

Caporael, Linnda R. "Ergotism: The Satan Loosed in Salem?" *Science* 192 (1976): 21-26.

Hansen, Chadwick. *Witchcraft at Salem.* New York: G. Brazilier, 1969.

Kittredge, George Lyman. *Witchcraft in Old and New England.* New York: Russell & Russell, 1956.

Silverman, Kenneth. *The Life and Times of Cotton Mather.* San Francisco: Harper & Row, 1984.

Starkey, Marion Lena. *The Devil in Massachusetts: A Modern Inquiry into the Salem Witch Trials.* New York: Knopf, 1949.

Williams, Charles. *Witchcraft.* New York: Meridian Books, 1959.

Woodward, W. E. *Records of Salem Witchcraft.* 1864; rpt., New York: B. Franklin, 1972.

NOTE: Please continue to read about events that occurred after the spring of 1692, which will yield significant additional information concerning the relationship of Cotton Mather to Salem witchcraft.

Jonathan Edwards and the Great Awakening

This case was prepared by Samuel Garrett

Jonathan Edwards, sitting quietly in his study, considered his response to the council that had decreed his separation from the Northampton Church. For some weeks the council had been considering his fate. Could he be reconciled with his opponents? Now, in June 1750, and by one vote, the council had asked Edwards to leave. The pastor reflected on the events that had led to the crisis; and he prepared to react.

Edwards had served the congregation in western Massachusetts for twenty-three years. He had led that Northampton congregation and others as well in a great awakening of true affection for God. He had brought new learning to bear upon the age-old faith, supporting Puritan Christianity, not contributing to its decadence but rather recalling it to true religious life.

The quarrel between the minister and the majority of his parishioners had been simmering below the surface for a long time. In December 1748 it flared out into the open. For four years before there had been no profession of faith by a new member seeking admission to the congregation. Now Edwards was unwilling to admit an applicant who was unwilling to make that profession. The church's standing committee in turn objected to Edwards's requiring a profession. At length he was able to bring the dispute to a decision. The council representing neighboring congregations voted five to four to recommend his dismissal, which his congregation promptly carried into effect.

EARLY LIFE

Jonathan Edwards was born in 1703, the son of the Reverend Timothy Edwards, minister at East Windsor, Connecticut, and his wife, Esther Stoddard, the "Northampton pope's" daughter (Jonathan being their only son, with four elder sisters, and six younger ones). When he was eleven years old, Jonathan wrote an essay on spiders at his father's request, and it was sent to a friend in Old England. The work indicates how the boy had closely watched the creatures and set down as carefully and fully as he could the results of his observations. He concluded his essay with two corollaries as reminders of how this whole phenomenon witnesses to the glory and goodness of God. This essay and a shorter discussion of rainbows help to explain why Jonathan Edwards went off to Yale College when he was thirteen years old. He graduated with the Bachelor of Arts degree in 1720 despite institutional trauma among Yale's leaders, and he continued his studies in theology there for two more years. In August 1722, he took charge of a Scottish Presbyterian church in New York City. The following year he returned to Connecticut. There he helped with the teaching at Yale for a time (since the college rector and tutor had both gone over to the "prelacy" of the Church of England). In 1726, Edwards took up his ministry at Northampton.

Some twenty years later Edwards drew up a record of what he felt important about those years between college and Northampton ministry. In this "Personal Narrative" he related the course of his own awareness of God and the "new dispositions and that new sense of things that I have since had." He told how as a boy he was much concerned about religious matters and duties, meeting for prayer with friends or by himself, building a booth in a swamp for a place of prayer or going off into the woods instead. His affections had seemed to be "lively and easily moved," and he had seemed to be "in my element when engaged in religious duties."

His convictions and affections, however, had eventually abated. During those college years Edwards remembered struggles over the ways of sin and the terror of hell. He had finally resolved to break off his "former wicked ways" and to seek salvation, "but without that kind of affection and delight which I had formerly experienced." Conflicts and struggle continued, along with objections to the "horrible doctrine" of God's sovereignty until he became reasonably convinced of the doctrine's validity.

The "Personal Narrative" tells a good deal about Edwards's experience in New York, his return to Connecticut, an illness in 1725, and events having to do with his resolve after coming to Northampton. He spoke of his delight in the holiness of God, his concern for the advancement of Christ's kingdom in the world, his "view . . . of the glory of the Son of God as Mediator between God and man, his grace and love . . . an excellency great enough to swallow up all thought and conception." The "view" (or vision) on this occasion (which he said occurred in 1737) "continued as near as I can judge about an hour." Edwards spoke also of his own sense of sinfulness, of his dependence on God's grace and strength, and a sense from time to time, as on a Saturday night in January 1739, of indeed being enabled "to walk in the way of duty, to do that which was right and meet to be done, and agreeable to the holy mind of God."

The time at which Edwards wrote the "Personal Narrative" is significant: in the months after January 1739 a new revival was to break forth. Apparently Edwards was subjecting himself to analysis of an experience that he knew many others had also undergone or could yet undergo—others for whom he had a pastoral responsibility and concern.

In July 1727, Edwards married Sarah Pierpont, five months after accepting the call of the Northampton Church to become the successor of his grandfather Solomon Stoddard. Sarah and Jonathan Edwards had eleven children.

EDWARDS AND BOSTON

Solomon Stoddard died in 1729, leaving Edwards as "heir" to the Northampton ministry. Two years later the young successor received his first challenge to show his abilities in the larger New England church community. Edwards was invited to deliver the Thursday lecture on 8 July 1731 at the First Church, Boston, where New England ministers could gather to hear each other preach (being unable to do so on Sunday) and to debate the points of New England Puritan theology which they in turn expounded. They now had the chance to see how well Stoddard's young grandson, educated at Yale instead of Harvard, could hold his own in the very center of New England theological learning and practice.

Edwards's journey to Boston and home again suggests a number of contrasts of which the ministers in his audience would have been well aware. For one, there was the traditional relationship of the Connecticut River Valley with its Western "frontier" life to Boston's prosperous urban society. And there was the corresponding emphasis of struggling Yale College on Puritan orthodoxy in contrast to established Harvard's more liberal interpretation of the Puritan way. Stoddard's distinctive view of Calvinist covenant theology (well-known and controversial) was set over against Boston's "free and catholick" latitudinarian theological stance. Increase and Cotton Mather, recently deceased, had deplored both deviations. Where would the young lecturer take his stand? With orthodoxy? With Stoddard's practical version of it? Or with the more urbane and tolerant world of Boston?

The title of Edwards's lecture gives a good idea of his stand at First Church, Boston: "God Glorified in the Work of Redemption, by the Greatness of Man's Dependence upon Him, in the Whole of It." The text was taken from 1 Corinthians 1:29-31: "That no flesh should glory in his presence. But of him are ye in Christ Jesus, who of God is made unto us wisdom, and righteousness, and sanctification, and redemption: that, according as it is written, He that glorieth, let him glory in the Lord." The theme of the lecture was that redemption is entirely and only the work of God, in which man in no way participates. Edwards here, in effect, threw down the challenge both to the Boston and to the North-ampton schemes of salvation: Boston's "free and catholick" view of a covenant, in which man's participation is rewarded with glory, and Northampton's sense of salvation, which no longer requires a covenant but instead leaves the issue susceptible to man's use of "converting ordinances." Edwards set both views aside, along with any other "schemes of divinity" similarly opposed to an absolute dependence upon God and thereby designed to diminish God's glory and "thwart the design of our redemption."

Something else in this Thursday lecture, which its hearers apparently could not as easily notice, told what kind of a Calvinist and what sort of a theologian Jonathan Edwards would be. In the course of his exposition of the text, Edwards distinguished the "objective good" that the redeemed have in God from the "inherent good" in which they also share. The objective good he defined as "that extrinsic object, in the possession and enjoyment of which [the redeemed] are happy": we may call it the *context* of redemption. He defined the inherent good as "that excellency or pleasure which is in the soul [of the redeemed person] itself": we may call it the *effect* of redemption upon the soul; it designates the experience of the redeemed.

Edwards then proceeded to describe the twofold quality of the inherent good, which consists of its excellency and pleasure. The redeemed "are beautiful and blessed by a communication of God's holiness and joy, as the moon and planets are bright by the sun's light, [and] the saint hath spiritual joy and pleasure by a kind of effusion of God on the soul." Faith, the traditional theological appropriation of this redemption by the soul, is ultimately understood as "a *sensibleness* of what is real in the work of redemption; and the soul that believes doth entirely depend on God for all salvation, in its own sense and act." Edwards laid down themes of his whole theological outlook. He betrayed, as he did to the Boston ministers, his awareness of the "new learning" of the Age of Reason which he and the Age alike were acquiring from the writings of Isaac Newton and John Locke.

Apparently Edwards had come across a copy of Locke's *Essay Concerning Human Understanding* in his early course at Yale College. According to Locke, the human mind in the real world apprehends reality first as sensible and then by reflection comes further to understand and to appreciate it. Thus, in his definition of the inherent good that the redeemed have in God, Edwards made use of Locke's psychology, which few had read in New England even by the time of the Boston lecture. "Excellency and pleasure" constitute the experience of God; therefore, "truth is in the seeing, not in the thing."

Edwards similarly drew on the perspective of Isaac Newton (to whom he had long before referred in his essay on the rainbow) in his incorporation of the new learning in his theology. The objective good, which the redeemed also have in God (the context of redemption), is that real world of the Newtonian discoveries, which Newton also affirmed to be the work of God and a witness to his excellence. An orderly and lawful universe, perceived as such by the information first of the senses and then by reflection, is the Lockean-Newtonian world in which Edwards was living. His work as a theologian dealt with that real world as he experienced it in 1731, during the "Age of Reason." And, as a theologian, Edwards affirmed God and the work of redemption to which Scripture, St. Augustine, and Calvin had borne witness wholeheartedly and without qualification, on behalf of that real, experienced world.

EDWARDS AND REVIVALISM

New England revivals soon demonstrated how Edwards went about making this affirmation. The earlier "awakening" of 1734-1735 was a Connecticut River Valley affair, the latest in a whole series of revivals that the preaching of Stoddard had brought to pass over the years but that had had no lasting effects or easily measured results. Two years after the 1735 revival had died down, Edwards published *A Faithful Narrative of the Surprising Work of God in the Conversion of Many Hundred Souls in Northampton, and Neighbouring Towns and Villages.* He expanded on a letter he had previously written about the revival as he tried to answer questions that certain London nonconformist ministers had on the subject. He discussed experiences in the small towns of western Mas-

sachusetts and Connecticut, presenting various "case studies." Among
them was the story of Phebe Bartlett of Northampton, four years old.
Phebe and her eleven-year-old brother had been talking of religious
matters, and the little girl seemed to take this much to heart, being
"observed very constantly to retire, several times in a day, . . . for
secret prayer."

> She once, of her own accord, spake of her unsuccessfulness, in that she
> could not find God, or to that purpose. But on Thursday, the last day of
> July, about the middle of the day, the child being in a closet, where it used
> to retire, its mother heard it speaking aloud, which was unusual, and never
> had been observed before; and her voice seemed to be as of one exceeding
> importunate and engaged, but her mother could distinctly hear only these
> words (spoken in her childish manner, but seemed to be spoke with ex-
> traordinary earnestness, and out of distress of soul) Pray BLESSED LORD
> give me salvation! I PRAY, BE pardon for all my sins! Her mother very
> earnestly asked her several times, what the matter was, before she would
> make any answer, but she continued exceedingly crying, and wreathing
> her body to and fro, like one in anguish of spirit. Her mother than asked her
> whether she was afraid that God would not give her salvation. She then
> answered yes, I am afraid I shall go to hell! Her mother then endeavoured
> to quiet her . . . till at length she suddenly ceased crying and began to
> smile, and presently said with a smiling countenance . . . Mother, the
> kingdom of heaven is come to me! . . .
>
> From this time there has appeared a very remarkable abiding change in
> the child: She has been very strict upon the Sabbath, and seems to long for
> the sabbath day before it comes, and will often in the week time be inquir-
> ing how long it is to the sabbath day, and must have the days particularly
> counted over that are between, before she will be contented. And she
> seems to love God's house . . . is very eager to go thither. Her mother once
> asked her why she had such a mind to go? Whether it was not to see the fine
> folks? She said no, it was to hear Mr. Edwards preach. When she is in the
> place of worship, she is very far from spending her time there as children at
> her age usually do, but appears with an attention that is very extraordinary
> for such a child. She also appears, very desirous at all opportunities, to go
> to private religious meetings, and is very still and attentive at home, in
> prayer time, and has appeared affected in time of family prayer. She seems
> to delight much in hearing religious conversation. When I once was there
> with some others that were strangers, and talked to her something of
> religion, she seemed more than ordinarily attentive; and when we were
> gone, she looked out very wistfully after us, and said . . . I wish they
> would come again! Her mother asked her why: Said she, I love to hear
> them talk!

The "Great Awakening" five years later was ushered into New England by the visit of George Whitefield to Boston in October 1740. His

stay in the province was brief. The next month he journeyed out to Northampton, down into Connecticut, and on to New York City. His impact, however, was immense, and frightening as well to many of the more "free and catholick" (as well as to the "prelatical" Church of England leaders). Edwards extended hospitality to Whitefield and became keenly interested in the Anglican revivalist's very different way of preaching. He noted its emotionalism and its often terrifying effects upon his hearers.

The Awakening from then on was in full progress. The following summer, ten years to the day after the Boston Thursday Lecture (8 July 1741), Edwards preached at nearby Enfield his best-known sermon, "Sinners in the Hands of an Angry God." The text was Deuteronomy 32:35: "Their foot shall slide in due time." Edwards's typical style was very unlike that of Whitefield: calm, even in tone, clearly modulated; he preached with his eyes fixed steadily on the rear of the church. Yet even with such a delivery, the effect of his sermon was such, with "a breathing of distress, and weeping," that Edwards "was obliged to speak to the people and desire silence, that he might be heard."

The sermon exemplified in a graphic way the wedding of Calvinist soteriology to Locke's psychology of sensation; the sinner's dire need for redemption was first brought home to the senses:

There are black clouds of God's wrath now hanging directly over your heads, full of the dreadful storm, and big with thunder; and were it not for the restraining hand of God, it would immediately burst forth upon you. The sovereign pleasure of God, for the present, stays his rough wind; otherwise it would come like a whirlwind, and you would be like the chaff of the summer threshing floor.

The wrath of God is like great waters that are dammed for the present; they increase more and more, and rise higher and higher, till an outlet is given; and the longer the stream is stopped, the more mighty and rapid is its course, when once it is let loose. . . . The bow of God's wrath is bent, and the arrow made ready on the string, and justice bends the arrow at your heart, and strains the bow, and it is nothing but the mere pleasure of God, and that of an angry God, without any promise or obligation at all, that keeps the arrow one moment from being made drunk with your blood. Thus all you that never passed under a great change of heart, by the mighty power of the Spirit of God upon your souls; all you that were never born again, and made new creatures, and raised from being dead in sin, to a state of new, and before altogether unexperienced light and life, are in the hands of an angry God. . . .

The God that holds you over the pit of hell, much as one holds a spider, or some loathsome insect over the fire, abhors you, and is dreadfully provoked: his wrath towards you burns like fire; he looks upon you as worthy of nothing else, but to be cast into the fire; he is of purer eyes than to bear to have you in his sight; you are ten thousand times more abominable in his eyes, than the most hateful venomous serpent is in ours. You have offended him infinitely more than ever a stubborn rebel did his prince; and yet it is nothing but his hand that holds you from falling into the fire every moment. It is to be ascribed to nothing else, that you did not go to hell the last night; that you was suffered to awake again in this world, after you closed your eyes to sleep. And there is no other reason to be given why you have not gone to hell, since you have sat here in the house of God, provoking his pure eyes by your sinful wicked manner of attending his solemn worship. Yea, there is nothing else that is to be given as a reason why you do not this very moment drop down into hell.

O sinner! Consider the fearful danger you are in: it is a great furnace of wrath, a wide and bottomless pit, full of the fire of wrath, that you are held over in the hand of that God, whose wrath is provoked, and incensed as much against you, as against many of the damned in hell. You hang by a slender thread, with the flames of divine wrath flashing about it, and ready every moment to singe it, and burn it asunder; and you have no interest in any Mediator, and nothing to lay hold of to save yourself, nothing to keep off the flames of wrath, nothing of your own, nothing that you ever have done, nothing that you can do, to induce God to spare you one moment. And consider here more particularly, *Whose* wrath it is: it is the wrath of the infinite God. . . .

And now you have an extraordinary opportunity, a day wherein Christ has thrown the door of mercy wide open, and stands in calling and crying with a loud voice to poor sinners; a day wherein many are flocking to him, and pressing into the kingdom of God. . . . How awful is it to be left behind at such a day! To see so many others feasting, while you are pining and perishing! To see so many rejoicing and singing for joy of heart, while you have cause to mourn for sorrow of heart, and howl for vexation of spirit! How can you rest one moment in such a condition? Are not your souls as precious as the souls of the people at Suffield, where they are flocking from day to day to Christ?

RELIGIOUS AFFECTIONS

After the Great Awakening in its turn had died down in western Massachusetts, Edwards preached a series of sermons in which he tried to evaluate the revival's impact. Later still he recast sermons into one of his most important theological works, *A Treatise Concerning Religious Affections,* published in Boston in 1746. Once again Edwards used a text from Scripture, 1 Peter 1:8: "Whom having not seen, ye love; in whom, though now you see him not, yet believing, ye rejoice with joy unspeakable and full of glory.'' The text is concerned with the manifestation of true religion in a time of persecution. That manifestation consists of love and joy in Christ. Edwards asserted that the burning question put by the revival—''What is the nature of true religion?''—could be answered in the same terms, explicating the text to make the point clear. True religion, he said, consists in great part of just such ''holy affections.'' How may one be able to judge in a time of religious revival where true religion is to be found? ''Holy affections'' had been from the beginning for Edwards the significant aspects of his own religious experience as well as of the experience of Sarah Pierrepont and Phebe Bartlett. The ''sense'' of love and joy, of sweetness and delight, ran throughout the story like a constant thread, and he proceeded to analyze and expound the practical importance of this view of religion in a time of great religious tension and uneasiness.

What is meant by ''affections,'' holy or otherwise, and how may one—indeed, *must* one—understand true religion in terms of them? Edwards began with the mind, or soul: the essential human person. He understood that the soul or mind, viewed from one aspect of human activity, had traditionally been designated as the ''understanding'' or intellect; he suggested that it could also be viewed as the ''inclination,'' or desire:

> God has indued the soul with two faculties: one is that by which it is capable of perception and speculation, or by which it discerns and judges of things; which is called the understanding. The other faculty is that by which the soul does not merely perceive and view things, but is some way inclined with respect to the things it views or consider; either is inclined to 'em, or is disinclined, and averse from 'em; or is the faculty by which the soul does not behold things, as an indifferent unaffected spectator, but either as liking or disliking, pleased or displeased, approving or rejecting. This faculty is called by various names: it is sometimes called the *inclination:* and as it has respect to the actions that are determined and governed by it, is called the *will:* and the *mind,* with regard to the exercises of this faculty, is often called the *heart.* . . . And it is to be noted, that they are these more vigorous and sensible exercises of this faculty, that are called the *affections.*

The affections are defined, therefore, as ''more vigorous and sensible exercises of the inclination and will of the soul,'' and it is with the ''holy affections,'' says Edwards, that true religion has to deal.

Although Edwards used the traditional term ''faculty'' to discuss the make-up of the human personality, his argument indicates that true religion is concerned with the whole person, the "mind" or "soul." True religion is concerned as well with what that whole person most ardently desires. As the 1731 Boston Lecture indicates, Edwards held that desire is met by God in redemption in terms of the objective good and the inherent good, and it is, of course, the inherent good in which the *holy* affections find their longing satisfied. It is, indeed, the grace of God that causes the holy affections, he suggests, and that brings them to good effect. This entails, however, that so much of the excessive and profitless emotion that the revival generated, much less the prudential self-seeking religion of "free and catholick" Arminianism, do not in fact belong to true religion, do not show that engagement of the affections that constitutes the love and joy in Christ of which the apostle speaks. They lack as well that last and most relevant sign of "holy affections" that is found in an ongoing Christian practice incorporating a godly obedience, awareness of goals, perseverance in living, and a sense of the Holy Spirit. A true revival of religion, Edwards argued, and the religion to which it gives birth would both issue in a stronger sense of religious devotion and ethical responsibility: where one's "treasure is, there will the heart be also."

In the postrevival breakdown of the 1740s at Northampton, Edwards tried to communicate the place of ongoing Christian practice in the lives of converted Christians. The people of Northampton for the most part preferred to slip back into their accustomed ways, into the "profession of godliness," or their "christless and graceless condition," or even simply the "beginnings of awakening" (as Edwards described them). Edwards's attempts to require a sincere profession of faith for church membership and a return in a sense to the older pre-Stoddardean Puritan sense of commitment were rejected. The charge that he was changing his grandfather's tradition into a tradition of more searching and uncomfortable pastoral care was the ostensible and understandable reason for his dismissal. Edwards believed more was at stake. He considered his alternatives and prepared to respond.

SELECTED BIBLIOGRAPHY

Edwards, Jonathan. *The Great Awakening: A Faithful Narrative*. Edited by C. C. Goen. New Haven: Yale University Press, 1972. This collection of Edwards's writings is volume 4 in a seven-volume series.

Gaustad, Edwin Scott. *The Great Awakening in New England*. New York: Harper & Row, 1957.

Heimert, Alan E., and Perry Miller, eds. *The Great Awakening: Documents Illustrating the Crisis and Its Consequences.* Indianapolis: Bobbs-Merrill, 1964.

Miller, Perry. *Jonathan Edwards.* New York: W. Sloane Associates, 1949.

Rutman, Dorrett Bruce, ed. *The Great Awakening: Event and Exegesis.* New York: Wiley, 1970.

Winslow, Ola Elizabeth. *Jonathan Edwards.* New York: Macmillan, 1940.

Isaac Backus and the Separation of Church and State

This case was prepared by Paul T. Dieffenbach

Elder Isaac Backus leaned back in the chair at his desk in Middleborough, Massachusetts, in early 1782 and let out a long sigh. For several weeks now Backus and the other Baptists in the state had been awaiting an opportunity to test in the courts the constitutionality of Article III of the recently enacted state constitution's Bill of Rights. The article approved the continuation in slightly altered form of the long-standing practice in Massachusetts of supporting by taxation the religious teacher chosen by each parish. The same article also guaranteed that no sect would be subordinated to any other. Being minorities in virtually all the parishes, the Baptists were compelled to furnish certificates attesting to their status as dissenters from the parish church. They viewed this as a mark of subordination to the parish church. Furthermore, they were opposed to religious taxation under any guise.

Backus's sigh was one of satisfaction, for he had just received word of a case that seemed to have all the necessary ingredients for testing the constitutionality of Article III. Elijah Balkcom, who regularly attended the Baptist church in Attleborough, had been hauled off to jail after refusing to pay a tax levied for the parish church (Congregational) and after refusing to furnish a certificate certifying that he attended the Baptist church. After finally deciding to pay his tax under protest, he consulted a lawyer and sued the tax assessors for damages, claiming he had been illegally taxed since it was unconstitutional for the assessors to require him to furnish a certificate, because Article III guaranteed that no sect should ever be subordinated to another. If Baptists were required to furnish certificates when they were in a minority in a parish, clearly they were being subordinated to the parish church. Backus was hopeful that this case might be the means whereby the Baptists would achieve the relief from religious taxation they had long sought.

THE BAPTISTS AND THE STANDING ORDER

Backus himself had once been a member of the Congregational church, having been born in 1724 into a respected Congregational family in Norwich, Connecticut. He was baptized as a child into the parish church and until his late teens he never questioned the orthodoxy of the parish church or its use of the halfway covenant, an arrangement whereby baptized adults who professed faith and led moral lives but who had not experienced conversion were accepted as members. Their children were baptized as "half-way" members and could not receive the Lord's Supper or participate in church elections. After his conversion in 1741 during the Great Awakening, Backus became disturbed at the large number of church members who were not visible saints. This led him to join in the formation of a separate church in 1745 that held conversion as a prerequisite for membership. He subsequently felt called to the preaching of the gospel, and after much soul-searching converted to antipedobaptist views and was rebaptized by immersion. He founded the First Baptist Church of Middleborough in 1756 and began a long career in the Baptist cause, with emphasis on the fight to overthrow what he viewed as an oppressive established system of Congregational churches in New England.

The year 1773 was a particularly significant one for the Baptists of Massachusetts, for it was in this year that the Baptists, at Backus's recommendation, began a program of civil disobedience in the matter of paying religious taxes. Prior to the enactment of the new state constitution in 1780, the Baptists, Quakers, and Anglicans, under the provisions of the royal charter and laws passed by the General Assembly of the colony, had been required to furnish certificates signed by the minister and three leading laymen of their congregation confirming their status as dissenters from the Standing Order—that is, the Congregational churches established by law in each parish. An individual presenting such a certificate to the tax assessor in his parish would be exempt from paying the tax required of all citizens in the parish for the support of the Congregational church. Yet the Baptists and other dissenting groups in Massachusetts were in a distinct minority, viewed as rabble-rousers by many. Hence the Congregational authorities in many parishes, by the use of dubious technicalities in the law and other means that the Baptists viewed as just plain unfair, often made it difficult if not impossible for the Baptists to obtain the exemptions to which they were entitled under the law.

In September 1772 Backus was chosen leader of the Grievance Committee and made an agent for the Baptists in the state by the Warren
Association, a voluntary fellowship of Baptist churches in the New England area that had been founded in 1767. Two more incidents in 1773
convinced Backus that the time had come for Baptists to practice civil
disobedience in the matter of paying religious taxes. In the town of
Mendon, authorities seized the goods of several Baptists because their
certificates did not explicitly say they were "conscientiously" of the
Baptist persuasion. In Chelmsford, three Baptists were taken to jail
because their certificates had been ignored by the assessors. In light of
these and other incidents, Backus called a meeting of the Grievance
Committee on 5 May 1773 to propose that Baptists forthwith refuse to
turn in any certificates; he hoped to place the authorities in the position of
having either to jail hundreds of Baptists or else do away with the
certificates.

At this same meeting, the association voted to publish a tract written
by Backus entitled "An Appeal to the Public for Religious Liberty." In a
later work, Backus summarized the reasons given in this tract for the
decision to withhold the certificates:

> 1. Because it implies an acknowledgement, that civil rulers have a right to
> set up one religious sect above another, which they have not. 2. Because
> they are not representatives in religious matters, and therefore have no
> right to impose religious taxes. 3. Because such a practice emboldens the
> actors therein to assume God's prerogative, and to judge the hearts of those
> who put not into their mouths. 4. Because the church is presented as a
> chaste virgin to Christ; and to place her trust and love upon any others for
> temporal support, is playing the harlot, and so the way to destroy all
> religion. 5. Because the practice above-said tends to envy, hypocrisy and
> confusion, and so to the ruin of civil society.

The response from this action was not all that Backus had hoped. At
his own church in Middleborough, where the Baptists had a strong following in the parish, the program worked quite well. Backus never again
issued certificates for members of his church, and though the parish
authorities threatened at first to seize their goods to pay the taxes if
certificates were not furnished, in the end the threats were never carried
out and the Baptists were exempted from the taxes without the certificates. Many other churches, however, left the issue up to the individual
members, issuing certificates to those who wanted them, and other
churches continued to issue them to all, so the net result of the action
proved indecisive.

THE APPROACHING REVOLUTION

The approaching Revolution provided different opportunities for the Baptists in their struggle. The Baptists eagerly adopted the slogans of the day for their own appeals for religious liberty. Yet, though the Baptists by and large came to support the Revolution whole-heartedly, their small numbers and their reputation as troublemakers precluded any significant role for them in such organizations as the Sons of Liberty, whose slogans they borrowed. Indeed, the Baptists viewed themselves as struggling for two sets of rights. As Backus would later write, "while the defence of the civil rights of America appeared a matter of great importance, our religious liberties were by no means to be neglected; and the context concerning each kept a pretty even pace throughout the war." Since their battle for religious liberty brought them up against the Standing Order, from whose ranks many of the leaders of the Revolution came, one can understand why the Baptists' reputations remained suspect even when their support of the Revolution became obvious.

Such a misunderstanding arose in 1774, when Backus was delegated by the Warren Association to attend the annual meeting of the Philadelphia Association of Baptist Churches and at the same time was asked to bring their grievances before the Continental Congress, which was meeting in the city at the same time. While the Congress had no legal authority over the Massachusetts colony, the Baptists were hoping that the assembly would be able to bring pressure to bear on the Massachusetts delegates to make peace with the Baptists in order to promote unity for the coming struggle against England. A special meeting was held between the Baptist delegates and the representatives from Massachusetts upon the advice of some Quakers who had joined the Baptists for the discussions. The resulting impolitic behavior of the Quakers at this meeting, however, led to reports circulated back in Massachusetts that the dissenters by coming to Philadelphia were attempting to disrupt the unity of the colonies and break up the Continental Congress. The neutral and in some cases loyalist political views of the Quakers were charged to the Baptists as well.

Backus was later able to undo the damage through a petition to the Massachusetts Provincial Congress in which he again argued that the Baptists, in fighting for religious liberty, were fighting for the same principles as the patriots were fighting for in the challenge to England. In the petition he stated that he had made the trip to Philadelphia only to seek the aid of Congress in assuring "the future welfare of our country." The Baptists, he concluded, were "ready to do all in our power for [the country's] general welfare." The reply received from the Congress informed the Baptists that the Congress had no power to act on their petition and recommended that they petition the next General Assembly of the colony, where they surely would receive due attention.

The result for the Baptists of all this activity, then, was considerable misunderstanding and little in the way of concrete achievements. Yet the "even pace" Backus later described was indeed maintained. The withdrawal of the Royal Governor following the Revolution served to invalidate the old charter, and subsequent attempts to frame a new state constitution provided the Baptists with their best opportunity yet to abolish the system of the established church and religious taxation.

THE MASSACHUSETTS CONSTITUTION, 1777-81

In May of 1777, the General Assembly appointed a committee to draw up a constitution for the state, and after some revisions by the legislature as a whole, sitting as a self-constituted constitutional convention, the document was sent to the towns for a vote. The proposed constitution contained no bill of rights and left the established religious system unchanged. At the next meeting of the Assembly, in 1778, the votes were to be counted and the constitution established or rejected.

Upon hearing of the contents of the proposed constitution, Backus called for a meeting of the Grievance Committee on 21 February 1778. It was decided to issue a protest in the form of a petition, obtain the signatures of as many subscribers as possible, and the present it to the legislature. The petition stated in conclusion that the Baptists' "earnest prayer is that your Honors may be the happy instruments of promoting such impartial peace, as to fix it as a fundamental principle of our constitution, that religious ministers shall be supported only by Christ's authority and not at all by assessment and secular force, which impartial liberty has long been claimed and enjoyed by the town of Boston."

As it turned out, however, the petition was never presented, because the towns' voters were overwhelmingly against the new constitution. Many protested the lack of a bill of rights and most were of the opinion that the legislature did not have the authority to make itself a constitution-making body. A constitutional convention, comprised of delegates elected from each town, would be needed to write a new body of law for the state.

Prior to the meeting of the assembly in May 1778 to look at the results of the voting, the Reverend Phillips Payson of the Standing Church in Chelsea delivered the annual election sermon. He supported the constitution as formed by the legislature, but more importantly in his sermon he warned against the dangers of allowing a system of voluntary support to replace the established ecclesiastical system. The public worship of God was of extreme importance to civil society and government, he said; "let the restraints of religion once be broken down, as they infallibly would be by leaving the subject of public worship to the humors of the multitude, and we might well defy all human wisdom and power to support and preserve order and government in the state."

Backus and the Baptists rightly perceived this as an attack upon them and their cause. Backus therefore prepared and by unanimous consent of the Warren Association published the following September a tract entitled "Government and Liberty Described, and Ecclesiastical Tyranny Exposed." He was justifiably proud of his efforts, for in the tract he quoted from an argument used eleven years before by Standing Minister Charles Chauncy in his attack on the proposal to establish an American episcopate. Chauncy had said,

> We are, in principle, against all civil establishment in religion. It does not appear to us that God has entrusted the state with a right to make religious establishments. . . . We are as willing [the Episcopalians] should possess and exercise religious liberty in its full extent as we desire to do it ourselves. But let it be heedfully minded we claim no right to desire the interposition of the state to establish that mode of worship, government, or discipline we apprehend is most agreeable to the mind of Christ. We desire no other liberty than to be left unrestrained in the exercise of our principles insofar as we are good members of society.

Backus asserted that Chauncy's position constituted an equally valid argument against the establishment now present in New England (although Chauncy obviously disagreed, since he saw "establishment" only in terms of the aspects enumerated above: worship, church government, and discipline). Chauncy and the other Standing Ministers were talking out of both sides of their mouths as Backus saw it; they would as readily agree with Payson as with Chauncy! Yet it was quite unclear to him, Backus argued, how one could be opposed to establishment of religion by the state while at the same time supporting such establishment in a different form. Backus said again that just as the colonies were not represented in the British Parliament that was determining their taxes, so religious groups were not fairly represented by the civil rulers of the colony. Liberty of conscience could not be rightly enjoyed until this inequity was removed. As for the argument that the restraints given by religion in preserving order in society would be broken down if religion was not supported by the state, he argued that one had only to look at

Boston, where by special exemption all churches in the town were already on voluntary support. Such a system was contributing to the welfare of the town, not injuring it. Backus concluded the tract with an appendix describing some of the recent incidents (such as those at Mendon and Chelmsford) in which the Baptists had been mistreated under the present system.

The tract evidently caught people's attention, for the General Assembly voted to ask Elder Samuel Stillman of the First Baptist Church of Boston to deliver the election sermon the following year. Thus it was that on May 26, 1779, Stillman delivered his sermon to the assembly, reiterating as reasonably as possible the Baptist arguments for the separation of civil and ecclesiastical affairs so that the Baptists would enjoy the same liberty of conscience and purity of religion as was afforded the Standing Order.

Back in Middleborough, Backus was elected to a committee charged with providing instructions for the town delegates to the convention. When their work was completed, Backus was able to note with some satisfaction in his diary that an article he had written and recommended, in which equal liberty of conscience was guaranteed, was received and accepted without alteration. Another such opportunity arose for Backus to express his views when the mail brought him a letter dated 20 July 1779 from his good friend Elder Noah Alden. Alden, pastor of the Baptist church in Bellingham, had been elected as a delegate to the convention from his town and sought Backus's advice as to what should be included in the bill of rights.

Backus responded by sending Alden a proposal for a bill of rights as he felt they should be spelled out (see Exhibit 1 on p. 40). Patterned after the Virginia Bill of Rights composed by George Mason and utilizing his reading of John Locke, Backus's "Declaration of the Rights of the Inhabitants of the State of Massachusetts, in New England" contained a clear statement of his views concerning the separation of church and state, asserting in part that "every person has an unalienable right to act in all religious affairs according to the full persuasion of his own mind, where others are not injured thereby." With this document in his friend's hands, Backus could be sure his views would be heard at the convention.

THE MASSACHUSETTS BILL OF RIGHTS AND RELIGION

The convention was convened 1 September 1779 at Cambridge with 293 delegates in attendance. A large committee was appointed to compose a tentative constitution, and they subsequently chose three members to work on it. The result was largely the work of John Adams. It fell to Samuel Adams, however, to compose the clauses in the bill of rights concerning religion. There was considerable debate over this article when the entire convention reconvened. The article gave the legislature the right to make laws concerning the support of religion, but made the allowance that each taxpayer could request that his payment be applied to the support of a teacher of his particular denomination. The convention could not reach a consensus on the matter.

The convention finally decided to have this article recommitted. To that end it appointed a committee of seven that included Backus's friend Noah Alden to restudy the matter and draw up a new article. The majority report of the committee (Alden and two others voted against it), which retained Adams's suggestions for the support of religion, was over-whelmingly approved by the convention. Yet, taken with other statements in Article III and some in Article II, the finished article seemed to be offering religious liberty while at the same time maintaining a form of establishment (see Exhibit 2 on p. 40). These ambiguities were to spark a lively debate. Indeed, public discussions over the new constitution began even before the convention voted on 2 March 1780 to send the proposed constitution to the towns for voter ratification. Each section of the constitution would have to receive the approval of two-thirds of the voters in order to be accepted.

The ensuing debate over Article III was largely confined to the issue of religious taxation. Both supporters and opponents of Article III were in agreement with the provision of Article II that the right to complete freedom in religious worship is unalienable and that the state has no right to abrogate it. In addition, both sides agreed with the last statement of Article III to the effect that no subordination of any one sect or denomination would ever be established by law. But the question of whether the government should be in the business of supporting the establishment of religion in general (i.e., Protestant religion) remained the source of considerable disagreement.

Much of the debate was carried on in the newspapers. Letters of varying degrees of fervor appeared in the various journals in support of both sides. Backus wrote several of these himself in response to letters that attacked him personally and took issue with his tracts on the subject. He was also asked to speak out in his role as agent for the Baptists. And he composed another tract on the subject in an additional attempt to sway the voters' minds.

The supporters of Article III believed that religion was extremely important for maintaining a free society because it reinforced many moral principles necessary for the well-being of society. They questioned whether religion could continue to serve that role if its support were left to the whims of individuals. As they saw it, state support of religion was just as necessary as state support of the judiciary, the public roads, and the armed forces. Taxes that supported each of these were part of the price to be paid for the general welfare of society.

Backus, on the other hand, considered the new system of general assessment for the support of Protestant religion to be worse than the old system of support for the Standing Order. The old tax exemptions for dissenters were now to be removed; all would be required to pay a tax. Moreover, all taxes paid would go to the teacher elected by the majority in each parish unless an individual could verify that he attended the teaching of another minister. It appeared as though the hated certificates would still be required in order to prove oneself a dissenter. Would this not in fact result in the subordination of the minority to the majority in each parish, in contradiction to the conclusion of Article III? In any event, the Baptist ministers could not in good conscience accept any support from the state, even out of the taxes paid by members of their churches. Backus summarized his opposition to Article III in a petition to the General Assembly.

We . . . enter our protest against the power claimed in the Third Article of the declaration of rights in the new plan of government introduced among us;—for the following reasons, viz.:

1. Because it asserts a right of the people to give away a power they had themselves; for no man has a right to judge for others in religious matters; yet this article would give the majority of each town and parish the exclusive right of covenanting for the rest with religious teachers, and so of excluding the minority from the liberty of choosing for themselves in that respect.

2. Because this power is given entirely into the hands of men who vote only by virtue of money qualifications. . . .

3. Because said article contradicts itself; for it promises equal protection of all sects, with an exemption from any subordination of one religious denomination to another; when it is impossible for the majority of any community to govern in any affair, unless the minority are in subordination to them in that affair.

4. Because by this article the civil power is called to judge whether persons can conveniently and conscientiously attend upon any teacher within their reach, and oblige each one to support such teachers as may be contrary to his conscience; which is subversive of the unalienable rights of conscience.

5. Because, as the convention say, "power without restraint is tyranny"; . . . and it is evident all these powers are united in the Legislature, who by this Article are empowered to compel both civil and religious societies to make what they shall judge to be suitable provisions for religious teachers. . . .

Thus, although the new constitution made it possible for a Baptist minister (or any other dissenting minister) to be elected as a parish minister without having to meet certain educational requirements, this concession was insignificant as a practical matter because of the Baptists' minority status in virtually all the parishes. Furthermore, their past experiences with the certificates made the Baptists skeptical that the new arrangement would be any more fairly administered even if their pastors were willing to accept the taxes paid by the members of their churches. In the end, the crux of the matter remained that the Baptists considered all religious taxation an unconscionable rendering to Caesar what was not Caesar's. To give certificate or religious tax was to give at least tacit approval to the contention that the state had the right to dictate in such affairs. Backus and the Baptists steadfastly maintained that this right belonged exclusively to Christ, the head of the church.

Despite all the arguments against Article III pressed by Backus and the others, the entire constitution was declared to have received the necessary two-thirds votes of approval when the convention reconvened in June 1780. Noah Alden reported to the Warren Association that by his count Article III had received a majority of the votes but not the necessary two-thirds. Nonetheless, the convention declared it approved and on 25 October 1780 the General Assembly declared the constitution to be the fundamental law of the state, thereby choosing to ignore the last petition by Backus and the Warren Association.

What had seemed the best opportunity afforded the Baptists for realizing their goal of complete disestablishment had passed. Within just a few weeks Backus and the Grievance Committee began receiving accounts of injustices suffered by Baptists under the new system. Since it was clear that any petitions to the legislature would fall upon deaf ears, Backus was convinced that the only remaining course of action available to the Baptists would be through the courts. They needed a case that would compel the courts to decide on the constitutionality of Article III in light of the assurance given in that article that no sect or denomination could lawfully subordinate any other, and the assurances of Article II of freedom of worship. Backus was hopeful that the Balkcom case would be what they were looking for.

Exhibit 1

Article 2 of Isaac Backus's Bill of Rights
("A Declaration of the Rights of the Inhabitants of the State of
Massachusetts-Bay, in New England")

2. As God is the only worthy object of all religious worship, and nothing can be true religion but a voluntary obedience until his revealed will, of which each rational soul has an equal right to judge for itself; every person has an inalienable right to act in all religious affairs according to the full persuasion of his own mind, where others are not injured thereby. And civil rulers are so far from having any right to empower any person or persons to judge for others in such affairs, and to enforce their judgments with the sword, that their power ought to be exerted to protect all persons and societies within their jurisdiction, from being injured or interrupted in the free enjoyment of this right, under any pretense whatsoever.

Exhibit 2

Articles II and III of the Bill of Rights of the Massachusetts Constitution, composed and ratified in 1780

II. It is the right as well as the duty of all men in society, publicly, and at stated seasons, to worship the SUPREME BEING, the great Creator and Preserver of the universe. And no subject shall be hurt, molested, or restraining in his person, liberty, or estate, for worshipping GOD in the manner and season most agreeable to the dictates of his own conscience; or for this religious profession of sentiments; provided he doth not disturb the public peace, or obstruct others in their religious worship.

III. As the happiness of a people, and the good order and preservation of civil government, essentially depend upon piety, religion, and morality; and as these cannot be generally diffused through a community but by the institution of the public worship of GOD, and of public instructions in piety, religion and morality: Therefore, to promote their happiness, and to secure the good order and preservation of their government, the people of this commonwealth have a right to invest their legislature with power to authorize and require, and the legislature shall from time to time, authorize and require the several towns, parishes, precincts, and other bodies politic, or religious societies, to make suitable provision at their own expense, for the institution of the public worship of GOD, and for the support and maintenance of public Protestant teachers of piety, religion, and morality, in all cases where such provision shall not be made voluntarily.

And the people of this commonwealth have also a right to, and do, invest their legislature with authority to enjoin upon all the subjects an attendance upon the instructions of the public teachers aforesaid, at stated times and seasons, if there be any on whose instructions they can conscientiously and conveniently attend.

Provided, notwithstanding, that the several towns, parishes, precincts, and other bodies politic, or religious societies, shall, at all times, have the exclusive right of electing their public teachers, and of contracting with them for their support and maintenance.

And all moneys paid by the subject to the support of public worship, and of the public teachers aforesaid, shall, if he require it, be uniformly applied to the support of the public teacher or teachers of his own religious sect or denomination, provided there be any on whose instructions he attends; otherwise it may be paid towards the support of the teacher or teachers of the parish or precinct in which the said moneys are raised.

And every denomination of Christians, demeaning themselves peaceably, and as good subjects of the commonwealth shall be equally under the protection of the law: and no subordination of any one sect or denomination to another shall ever be established by law.

SELECTED BIBLIOGRAPHY

Backus, Isaac. *A History of New England with Particular Reference to the Denomination of Christians Called Baptists.* 2 vols. 2d edition, with notes by David Weston. Newton, Mass.: Backus Historical Society, 1871.

Ford, David B. *New England's Struggles for Religious Liberty.* Philadelphia: American Baptist Publication Society, 1896.

Hovey, Alvah. *A Memoir of the Life and Times of the Rev. Isaac Backus,* A.M. Boston: Gould & Lincoln, 1858.

Maston, T. B. *Isaac Backus: Pioneer of Religious Liberty.* Rochester, N.Y.: American Baptist Historical Society, 1962.

McLoughlin, William G. *Isaac Backus and the American Pietistic Tradition.* Boston: Little, Brown, 1967.

_____. *New England Dissent, 1630-1833: The Baptists and the Separation of Church and State.* Cambridge: Harvard University Press, 1971.

_____, ed. *Isaac Backus on Church, State, and Calvinism: Pamphlets, 1754-1789.* Cambridge: Belknap Press, 1968.

John Woolman and American Slavery

This case was prepared by Douglas H. Gregg

Alone and in bed, he found that sleep would not come. The events of that day, the second day of the yearly meeting of the Society of Friends in Newport, 1760, were too fresh and vivid in John Woolman's mind: the arrival of a slave ship from Africa to Newport Harbor, the display of a large number of slaves for sale by a member of his society, the growing wealth and prosperity of the Friends reflected in dress and manner at the day's meeting . . .

In his travels John Woolman had often come upon evidence that the desire to get riches, live comfortably, and provide inheritances for children had entangled many in the spirit of oppression. Surely, he thought to himself, it should be clear that this trade in slaves is a great evil and tends to multiply troubles and bring distress upon both owners and slaves alike. But what to do?

EARLY LIFE

John Woolman was born in Northampton, Burlington County, New Jersey, some twenty miles east of Philadelphia on 19 October 1720. The fourth of thirteen children, he was raised in the simple environment of a farming family. His parents, pious and industrious Quakers, were of modest means but saw to it that their children were sent to school and given training in spiritual matters. On Sunday afternoons, the children would read aloud to one another from Holy Scripture or some religious book.

In this setting, Woolman's religious sensitivities were awakened early. By age seven, he "began to be acquainted with the operations of Divine Love." Reading after school one day from Revelation 22, he found his mind "drawn to seek after that pure habitation which . . . God had prepared for his servants." He concluded that people in his age seemed to live with "less steadiness and firmness" than those described in the Scriptures.

As an adolescent, Woolman was torn by conflicting forces. He wanted to share in the youthful obedience, frivolity, and vanities of his youthful companions, but he also wanted to "walk humbly" before God and pursue the demands of a serious religious vocation. Through persistence in attending Quaker meetings, reading the Scripture, and meditation, the latter desires were strengthened and the foundation for his life was established. He was early convinced that

> true religion consisted in an inward life, wherein the heart doth love and reverence God the Creator and learn to exercise true justice and goodness, not only toward all men but also toward the brute creatures; . . . to say we love God as unseen and at the same time exercise cruelty toward the least creature moving by his life, or by life derived from him, was a contradiction in itself.

At the age of twenty-one, Woolman left home and moved to Mount Holly, some five miles away, where he hired out to tend a retail store. Within a few years he set up shop for himself and gradually began to prosper without really intending to do so. Concerned that material success might disturb the balance in his life, he resisted the temptation to expand his business and instead cut back on his retail trade. He had learned "to be content with real conveniences that were not costly"; "a way of life free from much entanglements appeared best" to him, even though the income was small.

Woolman eventually gave up retailing altogether in favor of tailoring, which he could control more easily and which allowed him to live "in a plain way without the load of a great business." To supplement his income, he engaged in surveying, drawing up legal documents such as wills and deeds, teaching, tending orchards—whatever allowed him to live in an unhurried fashion and pursue his real calling. He was continually wary of success lest he fall into selfishness and "through loving this present world he be found in a continued neglect of duty with respect to a faithful labor for a reformation."

When Woolman was twenty-three years old, the monthly Quaker meeting of Burlington, New Jersey, recognized him as a minister—one whom the Lord had chosen for an occasional ministry of speaking in meetings when the Spirit prompted and traveling to other meetings to share convictions—and it was duly recorded in the minutes of the meeting. In subsequent years, Woolman made numerous journeys to Quaker settlements from New England to the Carolinas—journeys he faithfully recorded in a journal he kept for this purpose.

He married Sarah Ellis when he was twenty-nine. They had one daughter, Mary, who survived infancy. Those who knew John Woolman thought him a loving husband and tender father. His journeys took him away from home an average of a month each year, but he and Sarah were in agreement over the journeys, believing that so long as their decisions were in "the pure spirit of Truth" God would "be their guide and support."

Throughout his life, Woolman believed that "to turn all the treasures we possess into the channel of universal love becomes the business of our lives." He tackled a myriad of social problems—the effects of poverty, the treatment of laborers, the conditions of life at sea for seamen, the causes of war, and civil disobedience and conscientious objection in relation to war and taxes. His concern for the Indians caused him to undertake a hazardous, exhausting journey into the wilderness "that I might feel and understand their life and the spirit they live in, if haply I might receive some instruction from them." But of all the issues that confronted him, it was slavery that most troubled his conscience and consumed him in his travels and ministry. The channeling of universal love toward the abolition of slavery became the "business" of his life.

A QUICKENED CONSCIENCE

In 1743, while still clerking in the general store at Mount Holly, John Woolman was directed by his employer to write a bill of sale on a black woman whom the employer had just sold to a waiting buyer. It was a routine matter of everyday business, but it troubled John Woolman.

> The thing was sudden, and though the thoughts of writing an instrument of slavery for one of my fellow creatures felt uneasy, yet I remembered I was hired by the year, that it was my master who directed me to do it, and that it was an elderly man, a member of our Society, who bought her; so through weakness I gave way and wrote it, but at the executing it, I was so afflicted in my mind that I said before my master and the Friend that I believed slavekeeping to be a practice inconsistent with the Christian religion.

Woolman's conscience continued to trouble him; he wished that he had asked to be excused from writing the bill of sale, because it was against his conscience. A short time later a young man of the Society of Friends asked Woolman to write a similar document. Woolman declined, saying he "believed the practice was not right and desired to be excused from writing it."

In 1746, Woolman undertook a three-month journey to Friends in the back settlements of Pennsylvania and Virginia, venturing as far into the South as North Carolina and returning by way of Maryland. This was Woolman's first experience with the widespread practice of slavery, and it left him deeply troubled. Many evenings during the journey, Woolman would have free lodgings with families in the Society. During these times he observed that in some cases, the masters bore a good share of the burden of work and lived frugally so that their slaves were well provided for and their work was moderate, but it was more often the case that the masters lived in ease and luxury on the labor of their slaves and laid heavy burdens on them. This so troubled Woolman's conscience that he sought out the owners for private conversation regarding the practice of slavery. At the conclusion of the trip, he recorded in his journal, "I saw in these southern provinces so many vices and corruptions increased by this trade and this way of life that it appeared to me as a dark gloominess hanging over the land; and though now many willingly run into it, yet in future the consequence will be grievous to posterity."

This was not a passing notion for Woolman. It became, as he put it, a "matter fixed on my mind," and soon after returning from the South he wrote an essay entitled "Some Considerations on the Keeping of Negroes." Taking Matthew 25:40 as his text—"Forasmuch as ye did it to the least of these my brethren, ye did it unto me"—Woolman spoke with equal concern of the pain and suffering of the slaves and the corrupting laziness and greed of the slaveholders that was being passed on to their children. Some slaves, he noted, were well-treated, but this was an exception. Even good intentions were biased by narrow self-love, and few people had sufficient wisdom and goodness to warrant being entrusted with absolute power over others.

SECOND SOUTHERN JOURNEY—1757

During a second trip to the South in 1757, Woolman was determined to keep his actions as uncompromisingly pure in principle as he could. He knew that one's conduct was more convincing than one's language, so he decided not to accept kindness or hospitality during the journey that was in any way the result of the labor or oppression of slaves. Thinking this through in advance, he took along enough money to pay the slaves for lodgings offered him by their masters. When he left a household where he had been lodged and entertained, he would speak to the head of the family in private, giving him money and telling him to distribute it to his slaves; in some cases he gave the money directly to the blacks. He wanted to be free of any obligations to slaveowners, for he had in mind the biblical injunction in Exodus 23:8: ''Thou shalt not receive any gift; for a gift blindeth the wise, and perverteth the words of the righteous.'' This proved to be a trial both to Woolman and the slaveowners, whose behavior he was calling into question, but Woolman recorded later that ''the way was made easier than I expected, and few if any manifested any resentment at the offer, and most of them after some talk accepted of them.''

Early in this journey, Woolman happened in company with a colonel of the militia who seemed to Woolman to be a thoughtful man. Engaging him in conversation, Woolman remarked on the difference between people who work hard for their living, training their children in frugality and business, and those who live on the work of their slaves, the former life being the most happy in Woolman's view. The colonel concurred, mentioning the trouble that arose from the lazy disposition of the negroes, adding that a local laborer would do as much in a day as two slaves. Woolman replied, ''Free men whose minds were properly on their business found a satisfaction in improving, cultivating, and providing for their families, but Negroes, laboring to support others who claim them as their property and expecting nothing but slavery during life, had not the like inducement to be industrious.'' The colonel countered by saying that ''the lives of the Negroes were so wretched in their own country that many of them lived better here than there.'' The conversation ended there, but Woolman later responded to the same argument in the following manner:

> If compassion on the Africans in regard to their domestic troubles were the real motives of our purchasing them, that spirit of tenderness being attended to would incite us to use them kindly, that as strangers brought out of affliction their lives might be happy among us. . . . But . . . we manifest by our conduct that our views in purchasing them are to advance ourselves.

During this journey, Woolman learned that ''from small beginnings in error great buildings by degrees are raised.'' He noted more than once that as men of reputation depart from the truth, they are used as examples by the general populace to justify themselves in similar actions. Woolman realized more fully during this time the difficulties involved in overthrowing a system that was so firmly established economically and socially as to become a way of life.

PHILADELPHIA YEARLY MEETING—1758

The yearly meeting of Friends in Philadelphia, 1758, dealt with many weighty matters, including the proper relation of the church to those who purchase slaves. Of the members present, none openly justified the practice of slavekeeping in general, but several members were concerned that things might be said and discussed that would be discomfiting to many of the brethren and that the best course was to continue to pray that the Lord might open a way for the deliverance of the slaves. To this, John Woolman spoke, saying it was not a time for delay.

> Should we now be sensible of what he requires of us, and through a respect to the private interest of some persons or through a regard to some friendships which do not stand on an immutable foundation, neglect to do our duty in firmness and constancy, still waiting for some extraordinary means to bring about their deliverance, it may be that by terrible things in righteousness God may answer us in this matter.

Woolman felt that "the love of Truth in a good degree prevailed" at the meeting. Several Friends expressed their desire that visits be made to Friends who kept slaves, while others declared that they believed liberty was the negro's right. The meeting eventually adopted a formal minute "more full on that subject than any heretofore," urging Quakers to free their slaves, arranging for the visitation of slaveholders, and decreeing that any who bought or sold slaves were to be excluded from participating in the business affairs of the church. The way had been prepared for the abolition of slavery among all Quakers under the jurisdiction of the Philadelphia Yearly Meeting. But such work could not stop in Philadelphia or in Pennsylvania. Other Yearly Meetings would now have to face the same issue.

NEW ENGLAND YEARLY MEETING—1760

In the spring of 1760, Woolman journeyed into New England by way of New Jersey and Long Island. He arrived in Newport, one of the centers of the slave trade, in time for the New England yearly meeting. On the first day of the meeting, a slave ship had come into the harbor and a number of slaves were offered for sale by a member of the Society. A sense of the closeness of evil made Woolman shudder; he grew weak and trembled, experiencing the same sort of feeling that the prophet Habakkuk had spoken about: "When I heard, my belly trembled, my lips quivered, my appetite failed, and I grew outwardly weak" (Hab. 3:16).

Woolman believed some course of action was required. Could persuasion cause a merchant to set free several hundred weak and emaciated negroes in the face of his considerable investment? The legislature was then in session. There might be opportunity for Woolman to speak before the House of Assembly, but waiting for opportunity to speak might cause him to miss crucial discussions in the meeting regarding the selling and keeping of slaves. Perhaps a memorial might be prepared for the yearly meeting that could then be used to petition the Legislature to use its power to discourage the future importation of slaves. But how should such a memorial be phrased?

These and other thoughts flooded John Woolman's mind that evening as he tossed in bed, seeking sleep that would not come. He did not yet feel a satisfactory evidence in his own mind that a particular course of action was under the power of the cross of Christ. His whole life he had "gone forward, not as one travelling in a road cast up, and well-prepared, but as a man walking through a miry place, in which there are stones here and there, safe to step on, but so situated that one step being taken, time is necessary to see where to step next." He knew only that in time the next step would be clear, the Spirit would lead.

SELECTED BIBLIOGRAPHY

Cadbury, Henry J. *John Woolman in England: A Documentary Supplement.* London: Friends Historical Society, 1971.

Cady, Edwin H. *John Woolman.* Great American Thinkers Series. New York: Washington Square Press, 1965.

Drake, Thomas E. *Quakers and Slavery in America.* New Haven: Yale University Press, 1950.

Moulton, Phillips P., ed. *The Journal and Major Essays of John Woolman: A Library of Protestant Thought.* New York: Oxford University Press, 1971.

Rosenblatt, Paul. *John Woolman.* New York: Twayne Publishers, 1969.

Shea, Daniel B., Jr. *Spiritual Autobiography in Early America.* Princeton: Princeton University Press, 1968.

Part Two
Early Nation

After the adoption of the American Constitution, most Christian communions flourished in an atmosphere of freedom and support. In fact, the story of Christianity in America's early national period is first of all the story of growth. Churches existent at the time of the Revolution increased immensely both in numbers and in terms of denominational stability. New communions emerged into the mainstream in American religious life. Sects and communitarian movements proliferated, challenging the hegemony of established denominations.

Meanwhile, the number and quality of reforming efforts also increased, expressions of the growing confidence of American Christians that the kingdom of God would indeed come on earth as it was in heaven. At the same time, the structure and problems of American society grew more complex increasing the need for reforms. Even the setting, the sheer geography of "settled" America expanded rapidly. Its size doubled and quadrupled between 1790 and 1860.

Church membership figures reflect the incredible growth and change taking place generally. For example, Methodists numbered but a few thousand faithful in 1776, and perhaps no more than 70,000 in 1800, but by the time of the Civil War, Methodists North and South estimated their membership at more than 2,000,000. Baptists of various persuasions probably multiplied their rolls ten times over during the same period— from 100,000 adults to more than a million. Less spectacular but still dramatic gains occurred in the Presbyterian, Congregationalist, and Episcopalian churches. The growth was attributable both to the large numbers of conversions and to significant immigration from England, Germany, Holland, and Ireland.

Immigrants brought strength to communions that had not shared much of the incipient pluralism of the Revolution era. German Lutherans came, as did Scandinavians in large numbers after 1830. During this period, they frequently remained in tight-knit ethnic communities, retaining their separate languages and many of the other features of life characteristic of their previous communities. But on the frontier especially, they became an identifiable portion of the religious spectrum.

Roman Catholics had lived freely in only a few portions of colonial America, but during the early decades of the nineteenth century they moved into every state and almost every territory of the nation. Historian Edwin Gaustad estimates that there were almost three million American Catholics by the time of the Civil War. In addition to the immigrants from several countries that shared allegiance to Roman Church authority, some prominent Americans converted to Catholicism—Orestes Brownson, the spiritual pilgrim; Isaac Hecker, who founded the Paulist Society; and Edgar P. Wadhams, who became a bishop in the church to which he moved.

New denominations and sects emerged in the U.S. to pluralize further a religious spectrum already rich with a variety of Old World communions. The Disciples of Christ, or "Christian Church," gathered dissidents from among the Reformed bodies and the Methodists to form a communion out of an ecumenical movement. They sought to unite all Protestantism behind the principle that "where the Scriptures speak, we speak; where the Scriptures are silent, we are silent." The winsomeness of the movement and the forcefulness of the personalities of some of its leaders led hundreds of thousands to join.

Blacks led by Richard Allen gathered to form the African Methodist Episcopal Church, which sought religious autonomy in a world that would not yet grant social or political freedom. Black Baptist churches arose, often for the same reason—the desire for freedom.

Though they eschewed the designation "Protestant," the Church of Jesus Christ of the Latter Day Saints, or Mormons, grew to become a significant denomination early in the nation's history. A quasi-utopian community under the direction of Joseph Smith at its beginning, the Mormons moved gradually westward seeking places where they would be free to chart their own destiny. First into Ohio in 1831, then on to Missouri, Illinois, Nebraska, and finally to Salt Lake in 1857, the Mormons migrated to discover at last a "place in the sun."

Shakers, Rappites, Oneidans, and members of scores of other communities took their own faith seriously while at the same time challenging the ways of the Christian mainstream. Most of the communistic societies expected the imminent return of Jesus Christ in all his glory; some even proclaimed that the end of time had begun. They sought to embody the new creation in social relationships and economic systems of various kinds. Some less eschatological communitarians simply wanted to reform traditional ways of living, as did the followers of Robert Owen in New Harmony, Indiana, and the Icarians in Iowa.

Thus the number of denominations clearly multiplied phenomenally during this period. But growth entails more than mere numerical increase and expansion. Denominational consolidation also occurred, establishing many patterns of American church life that still prevail. In 1789 in Philadelphia, American Anglicans organized the "Protestant Episcopal Church" with Samuel Seabury of Connecticut, William White of Pennsylvania, and Samuel Provvost of New York as duly consecrated bishops. They adopted a prayer book distinctly different from that of the Church of England. The Episcopal Church was still concentrated on the eastern seaboard during this period; nevertheless, the denomination sent missionaries and members inland to begin Episcopal communities in other states. The church moved toward becoming a thoroughgoing American denomination.

Baptists, for the most part evangelical Calvinists during colonial times, grew to accommodate divergent theologies during the early national era. Some turned increasingly toward sectarian isolation and the idiosyncrasies of one-issue theologies. But most of the Baptists emphasized their distinctive beliefs as a portion of American religion and sought cooperation with the whole spectrum of Protestant mainstream churches. In so doing, the Baptist churches flourished.

Questions of reform and forces opposing reform fairly dominated the religious climate in the U.S. during this period. Ralph Waldo Emerson, the Unitarian minister turned essayist, claimed in 1841 that "in the history of the world the doctrine of Reform never had such scope as at the present hour." Both partisans of reform and those seeking the "good old days" probably would have agreed with the assertion.

Temperance, peace, literacy, respect for the Lord's Day, establishment of city parks, humanization of prisons and asylums for the mentally ill, missions, women's rights, and anti-slavery—all these causes drew Americans into reform movements. Protestant activism and the reaction to it expressed in doctrines of "the spirituality of the church" have remained characteristic expressions of the communions ever since. Protestant nativism—the movement to rid America of Catholicism—arose to become another more or less permanent fixture of the "spectrum of reform." Pro-slavery forces, which at first apologized for their efforts and subsequently attacked most other aspects of reform, attained a peculiar position in the spectrum. Apologists for slavery frequently saw abolition as a "retrogression" in the march of human civilization.

The goals of some reformers contradicted those of others, as, obviously, in the case of rift between those favoring slavery and those campaigning for abolition. Proponents of Christian pacifism parted ways with those who advocated war either to extend the influence of the United States "for Christianization of Mexico" or to abolish slavery in the South. Advocates of women's rights were accused of working against more important reforms such as abolition; those seeking prohibition were accused of working against the extension of human freedom. About the only ground common to all reformers was their appeal to conscience and religious principles of one form or another.

Abolition lay at the center of the reform movements. It produced an opposite reaction that split the Christian communions and divided the country itself. Early sentiment against the South's "peculiar institution" had been voiced in the slave-owning areas, especially in favor of gradual manumission by the American Colonization Society. But as the raising of cotton became increasingly profitable, as the technology for processing it improved, and as more strident cries for immediate abolition grew, Southerners with few exceptions defended slavery as at least a temporary measure by which to "civilize and Christianize Afro-Americans." Christian writers in the South cited biblical authority for the maintenance of the system of slavery. The Hebrew people were made slaves, and they subsequently made slaves of others, ran the argument. Noah had consented to slavery after God's judgment on "the sons of Ham," whom the proponents of slavery assumed to be the African peoples. In the New Testament, Jesus did not condemn it, and Paul sent Onesimus back to his owner, Philemon.

Anti-slavery reformers also pointed to specific proof texts in their rebuttal. In Christ there was to be "no slave," and Philemon was directed to receive Onesimus as "brother." Slavery demeaned all portions of the Christian church and inhibited freedom in Christ. Differences concerning abolition may well have contributed to the split between Old and New Schools of Presbyterianism that occurred in 1836 and 1837. Certainly the 1844 Methodist schism into Northern and Southern churches took place because of the belief on the part of some that slave-owners should not be permitted in positions of ecclesiastical authority. Many argued that slave-owners ought not even to be permitted to take communion. Baptists followed suit with a regional division the following year. One Lutheran body also parted its membership on account of slavery, as did the Episcopal Church and both "Schools" of Presbyterianism. American Christians who themselves were black—some slave, some free—embodied that same ambiguity, although most sought an immediate end to the institution.

It was during this period that Christianity in its institution developed what has aptly been described as "an American pattern." Many of the hymns now termed "old favorites" were introduced and accepted. Even such things as the tradition of placing of flowers in the nave and chancel of sanctuaries probably originated during the middle 1800s. And two important and distinctly American institutions sprang almost full-grown from the head (or was it the heart) of Christianity at this time—the revival and the theological seminary. Both have exercised profound influence on the life of the church ever since.

In the West, James McGready began to gather the faithful and the curious to camp meetings at the turn of the century. These occasions of prayer and preparation, "preachin' and singin'," built up to a protracted communion service as the emotional pinnacle of the entire experience. While "surprising works of God" had been experienced in the colonial "Great Awakening," the camp meetings and extended revivals were specifically designed to generate religious experience and produce conversions of the unchurched. Other Presbyterians such as Richard McNemar followed suit, especially in Kentucky. Ecumenically minded, they included Methodists and Baptists in the area as partners. Thousands gathered, perhaps as many as twenty thousand in 1801 at Cane Ridge under the leadership of Barton Stone, to partake in the preaching and eucharist.

Presbyterians soon split into Cumberland and Christian movements over proceedings in which some sought to suppress the fervor of the revivals. Methodists and Disciples of Christ in particular institutionalized the camp meeting, and along with Baptists and others they made the revival a part of American Christianity. The growth in revivals helped also to "soften" classic Calvinism. Lyman Beecher and Asahel Nettleton provided just two examples of this "New Divinity" in action.

The growth of revivals soon produced a coterie of professionals who "specialized in saving the 'lost' and motivating the 'redeemed' to good works." Elder Jacob Knapp on behalf of the Baptists, Edwards Norris Kird on behalf of the Congregationalists, and Charles G. Finney on behalf of all communions sought to induce religious experience with tried and true methods. Finney, by most accounts the most formidable of the revivalists, began his ministry as a Presbyterian, but he found the connectional church too stifling for his energies and eventually began to organize churches of congregational polity around his powerful personality. He also led for almost four decades the growth of Oberlin College in Ohio (1835-75). A portion of each year he led revivals in various places in the United States and the British Isles. Finney managed to mix nicely the call for conversion and the plea for reform of societal structures. Drawing on a mixture of Arminianism and Calvinism, he preached that all persons had a God-given ability to choose to live as Christians.

As significant a force as Finney was in the growth of revivalism, he also helped stimulate the growth of America's other new institution—the theological seminary. The American seminary began with Andover Theological Seminary, established in 1808 by the Congregationalists. Reacting to the "triumph" of Unitarianism at Harvard, the evangelical wing of the church representing Old Calvinism and the adjustments contributed by Samuel Hopkins united to found one school. It was Jedidiah Morse who argued that it should be called a "theological seminary" and receive for study only young men who had already completed college. Morse likewise lobbied for the school to offer a broad course of study, with a faculty of at least three members all teaching specialties. Andover began with hopes for three faculty and fifteen students at a time who would follow a three-year curriculum. Almost immediately their dreams were realized many times over; they had a student body of about one hundred right from the beginning cycle.

Andover was formed by the church to serve the needs of the denomination. Its board of governors required professors to pledge their allegiance to the doctrine of the communion and sought to admit as students only those who were pious members of the church—measures designed to insure the orthodoxy of instruction and the devotion of graduates to the ministry in congregations. They received handsome endowment funds to underwrite the costs of the process.

The immediate success of Andover inspired the Congregationalists to try to establish additional seminaries on the same model. Dutch Reformed Christians also emulated Andover when they set up a seminary in New Brunswick, New Jersey. Presbyterians modeled a refurbished Princeton program for ministerial education along the lines of the school in Massachusetts. This wing of Reformed Christianity had seminaries soon afterward in Virginia, South Carolina, Ohio, and Kentucky. attempts were also made at several other locations. It was a seminary— Lane in Cincinnati—to which Lyman Beecher moved from Boston as part of a concerted strategy to win the West for evangelical Christianity.

Unitarians claimed a distinctive seminary at Harvard. Episcopalians began a General Seminary in New York, to which city it returned after a brief and partial sojourn in New Haven; they also started up a school in

Alexandria, Virginia. The German Reformed Church established their seminary at Mercersburg, Pennsylvania. The Lutherans established one nearby at Gettysburg. The Baptists at Newton had a seminary, too. All these seminaries offered some assurance of stability for church life in the respective denominations.

Protestant and Catholic missions continued during America's early nationhood. Missionaries such as Cram sought to convict and convert America's indigenous population, though increasingly assertive native Americans frequently responded with skepticism, as did Red Jacket. Missions also continued for other segments of America's population as the nation moved inexorably toward civil war.

Richard Allen and the Birth of the African Methodist Episcopal Church

This case was prepared by Ronald C. White, Jr.

It was Sunday morning in 1792. Richard Allen, a young black Methodist, went as was his custom to worship at St. George's Methodist Episcopal Church in Philadelphia. Arriving just after the service had begun, he and his friends were directed by the sexton to seats in the gallery. Blacks had formerly sat around the wall on the main floor of the church, but the expansion they helped create had relegated them to the gallery. The increase was due in no small measure to Allen's efforts as a black preacher in the city.

Allen and his friends took seats toward the front of the gallery above the seats they had formerly occupied. Just at that moment the elder began to lead the congregation in prayer. Allen described what happened next.

> We had not been long upon our knees before I heard considerable scuffling and low talking. I raised my head up and one of the trustees, H———— M————, having hold of the Rev. Absalom Jones, pulling him up off his knees, and saying, "You must get up—you must not kneel here."
>
> Mr. Jones replied, "Wait until the prayer is over."
>
> Mr. H———— M———— said, "No, you must get up now, or I will call for aid and force you away."
>
> Mr. Jones said, "Wait until prayer is over, and I will get up and trouble you no more."
>
> With that he beckoned one of the other trustees, Mr. L———— S———— to come to pull him up. By this time prayer was over, and we all went out of the church in a body, and they were no more plagued with us in the church.

The question now was what to do. Going out from St. George's was the act of an oppressed people seeking liberation. It was a decisive step, but where would it lead?

CONVERSION AND CALLING

Richard Allen was born 14 February 1760 in Philadelphia. He was a slave to Benjamin Chew, a prominent lawyer who would become Chief Justice of the Commonwealth of Pennsylvania in the years before the Revolution. Sometime around 1768 the entire Allen family was sold to Stokeley Sturgis, who owned a farm near Dover, Delaware.

During Allen's teenage years Methodist circuit riders arrived in Delaware. Allen went along one day in 1777 to a typical service in the woods near the farm. Here he heard persuasive preaching that spoke both of God's boundless grace and of individual responsibility. He would recall what happened many times in the future.

> I was awakened and brought to see myself, poor, wretched, and undone, and without the mercy of God must be lost. Shortly after, I obtained mercy through the blood of Christ, and was constrained to exhort my old companions to seek the Lord.

Allen joined the Methodist Society. Methodism was in its infancy in these years. Francis Asbury, Thomas Coke, and other early Methodist itinerants observed that blacks were especially receptive to the proclamation of a gospel that stressed heart religion and plain doctrine. John Wesley's anti-slavery views were attractive to Richard Allen and other Afro-Americans. Blacks constituted a significant percentage of the growing Methodist membership in New York, Philadelphia, Baltimore, and Charleston in the last two decades of the century.

Allen now began to spread the news of his conversion. He wanted to convince others of the meaning and joy of the Christian life. First his mother and then his brother and sister were converted. Allen not only reached out to his relatives and friends but began to pray for his master. Neighbors told Sturgis that the religion his slaves were getting would contribute to the ruin of the plantation. Allen answered not by neglecting his duties but by organizing the slaves to work beyond their regular hours so that the output of the plantation was increased.

One day Allen asked permission to invite some of the Methodist preachers to the house. On one such occasion Freeborn Garrettson came to the Sturgis home. Garrettson had freed his own slaves in 1775. That day he preached on the text, "Thou art weighed in the balance and art found wanting." The implication of the text for slaveholding was proclaimed forcefully. Allen's master was converted and decided to free his slaves. In debt himself, Sturgis wrote up a manumission document that allowed Allen to work until he could pay for his freedom.

During the years of the American Revolution Allen worked at a variety of jobs. But his real love was preaching. When peace came, he began an itinerant ministry that took him as far south as South Carolina and as far north as New York. Sometimes he traveled alone and sometimes with white preachers.

THE FREE AFRICAN SOCIETY

Allen came to Philadelphia in 1785 in response to an invitation to preach to the black members of St. George's Church. But the burden of Allen's ministry was to seek out blacks who had not yet been touched by the gospel. At that time Philadelphia had a black population of about sixteen hundred—almost six percent of the total population. Though a few blacks were successful economically, most worked as laborers, mechanics, teamsters, seamen, and domestics. Most were unchurched.

In the spring of 1787 Allen's concern for the urban free blacks led to the formation of the Free African Society. The American Revolution had proclaimed liberty for all, but northern blacks knew from bitter experience that they did not possess the rights of a free people. Rather than be content with white benevolence, the Free African Society was begun as a mutual aid society and a nondenominational religious association. The society became a vehicle for black solidarity and planning for the future.

But the Free African Society could not ultimately meet the spiritual needs of its members. Allen's strong Methodist leanings were not appreciated by the society. Within two years he had quit it and it had quit him, suspending his membership.

Allen left the Free African Society determined to be involved in a church where blacks could control their own destiny and also worship as Methodists. This vision was present before the incident at St. George's; the walkout simply transformed a desire into an imperative.

THE BEGINNINGS OF BETHEL

Funding for a new church was critical. From the outset Allen was aided in a public subscription campaign by Benjamin Rush, a Presbyterian physician and philanthropist, and Robert Ralston, a white business leader. Both were members of the state abolitionist society. Allen said of his friends, "I hope the names of Dr. Benjamin Rush and Robert Ralston will never be forgotten among us. They were the first two gentlemen who espoused the cause of the oppressed."

The plans became a reality when a storeroom was rented as the first place of worship. Allen then purchased an abandoned blacksmith shop for $35 and hauled it with a team of six horses to the corner of Sixth and Lombard Streets. He dug the first spade of dirt as friends labored to renovate the building for its new purpose.

If there were a few whites who rallied to Allen's side, there was also much opposition. The criticisms were particularly hard to take when they came from the Methodist church itself. White Methodists harassed Allen at every turn. They threatened to dismiss all black Methodists who did not remove their names from the subscription lists. Allen replied that the fidelity of blacks to Methodist doctrine and discipline spoke for itself and argued that the way they were treated at St. George's necessitated their initiative to build their own church.

The new church was dedicated on 29 July 1794. Bishop Asbury preached the service. The presiding leader, John Dickins, prayed that this church might become a Bethel—a house of God—that would bring in "thousands of souls." Then and there the church became the Bethel African Methodist Episcopal Church.

CONTINUING CONTENTIONS

The contentions within Methodism did not go away. St. George's founded its own black chapel, Zoar, in 1796, but it was based on the principle of white control. Bethel insisted on control of its own affairs. The white Methodists argued that their polity called for denominational control of all property. The black worshipers at Bethel stated that they had raised their own funds for the church. All this time the black membership in Methodism was gaining much more rapidly than the white membership.

In 1796 an assistant minister at St. George's, Ezekiel Cooper, seemingly changed course by offering to assist Bethel in drawing up a document of incorporation. Bethel later learned that the document, while helpful in some ways, had at the same time assigned control of the property to the conference. Allen commented that the new church "belonged to the white conference, and our property was gone."

The simmering conflict came to a head in 1805, when James Smith was appointed elder in charge at St. George's. Examining Bethel's charter, he decided he was authorized to preach and administer the sacraments at Allen's church—and be paid for doing so. A collision occurred when Smith, according to Allen, "waked us up by demanding the keys and books of the church, and forbid us holding any meetings except by orders from him.''

This was the last straw. Allen determined that a solution must be found. Consulting a lawyer, he learned that the original charter could be amended by a two-thirds vote of the congregation. A so-called ''African Supplement'' to the first charter was adopted—and now the white elder claimed he had been deceived.

The African Supplement helped Bethel realize its desire to control its own affairs, but it did nothing to slow the continuing deterioration in relations with the white Methodist conference. The issue was clearly drawn. Black Methodists did not want to leave the larger Methodist denomination, but they did want to control their own affairs. White Methodists did not want the blacks to leave, but they insisted that ultimate control must lie within the conference.

A NEW DENOMINATION

In 1816 the issue of the charter and the African Supplement was decided by the courts. On the first of January the Court ruled in favor of Bethel. They were, in effect, legally recognized to be an independent body.

But now a new decision had to be faced. The story of the Bethel Church in Philadelphia was dramatic but not altogether unique. Black Methodists in Baltimore were involved in a similar struggle with white church leaders. Daniel Coker, pastor of the Bethel Church in Baltimore, preached a victory sermon on 21 January 1816, comparing the victory of the Philadelphia congregation to the return of the Jews from captivity in Babylon. Allen was aware of conflicts in Baltimore and other places. He now issued an invitation to meet a number of congregations in Philadelphia to discuss mutual problems.

On 9 April 1816, delegates from five congregations (from Baltimore; Wilmington, Delaware; Salem, New Jersey; Attleborough, Pennsylvania; and Philadelphia) met in response to Allen's initiative. Congregations in New York and Charleston did not send delegates but communicated their interest in the proceedings. Each of the congregations could bear testimony to discriminatory treatment at the hands of white societies. But all were indebted to their Methodist heritage.

Richard Allen was in the center of the discussion. He had fought a long battle for the independence of his congregation, but did this mean there should be an independent denomination? He know that other younger leaders were looking to him for direction. He pondered what to say and do.

SELECTED BIBLIOGRAPHY

Allen, Richard. *The Life Experience and Gospel Labors of the Rt. Rev. Richard Allen.* Nashville: Abingdon Press, 1960.

George, Carol V. R. *Segregated Sabbaths, Richard Allen and the Emergence of Independent Black Churches, 1760-1840.* New York: Oxford University Press, 1973.

Raboteau, Albert J. "Richard Allen and the African Church Movement," in *Black Leaders of the Nineteenth Century.* Edited by Leon Litwack and August Meier. Urbana, Ill.: University of Illinois Press, forthcoming.

Sernett, Milton C. *Black Religion and American Evangelicalism.* Metuchen, N.J.: Scarecrow Press, 1975.

Singleton, George A. *The Romance of African Methodism: A Study of the African Methodist Episcopal Church.* New York: Exposition Press, 1951.

Wesley, Charles H. *Richard Allen: Apostle of Freedom.* Washington: Associated Publishers, 1935.

Young, Henry J. *Major Black Religious Leaders, 1755-1940.* Nashville: Abingdon Press, 1977.

The Kentucky Revival

This case was prepared by Darrel M. Robertson

At the beginning of the nineteenth century, Richard McNemar perceived that "extraordinary outpourings of the Spirit of God" were falling upon people in the state of Kentucky. He was serving a small Presbyterian church in Cabin Creek, Kentucky, at the time.

McNemar had begun his ministry in western Pennsylvania. As a conservative Presbyterian, he had been taught to revere the eternal God and to farm for his livelihood. But McNemar's structured life was soon disturbed by great religious events that began about 1800 in Kentucky. The outbreak of "revival" throughout the state occasioned a crisis for many of the Presbyterian ministers. Young pastor McNemar shared their struggle. Was this frontier "revival" truly a work of God? Or was it the work of the devil, afflicting the religious with confusion and chaos?

THE STATE OF RELIGION: KENTUCKY

When Richard McNemar left his Pennsylvania parish and moved to Kentucky near the end of the eighteenth century, he found a generally discouraged group of believers in the new area. On 5 September 1796 McNemar received a letter from a fellow clergyman in Lexington:

> Dear Brother—It is not likely I can say anything to entertain or refresh you. I sometimes think I would be willing to travel with you to heaven, but I feel very unlike an inhabitant of that place. I would be glad to be at the truth and the substance.
>
> But I commonly feel so much more like a Devil than a Christian, that it makes me often forebode the displeasure of God, the Holy, and the Just. I sometimes think I am coming toward the birth, but I can seldom think I am born. O how long! How Long! And what am I? I would strip off everything but Christ and his Holy Spirit, to enter the narrow gate.

> I can tell you but little about my poor congregations. I see but little
> prospect of encouragement. I dare say none.
> I sometimes hope to see Jesus King in Zion.

Even more distressing to McNemar were those Christians who felt no
remorse at the unfortunate state of affairs. It pained him to observe how
they worked to condemn one another and to defend their own partisan
groups. He knew Christians were supposed to be united in heart and soul,
that they were supposed to lay aside all anger, wrath, envy, and evil talk.
Christians were supposed to be "kindly affectioned" one to another and
to love one another with a pure heart. But their actions proved clearly that
those who called themselves by the name of Christ were "full of envy
and strife, hateful and hating one another: and in every sense different
from those holy men of God, who are called by the name of Christ."

The problem, McNemar was convinced, was equally evident among
the clergy. The New Testament represented the ministers of Christ as
meek, humble, honest men—examples to their flocks. But what
McNemar saw were for the most part men who seemed proud, aspiring,
and contentious, eager for big salaries and government positions. Most
looked on common people as inferior beings. Some ministers even
owned slaves, which they sold for profit. In McNemar's eyes such men
could not be ordained of God, sustained by the Holy Spirit, or safely
believed or followed.

During the barren pre-revival years, McNemar took note of "praying
societies" which sprang up in different parts of the state. These groups
"professed to be in search of the truth and power of religion, and ready to
embrace it whenever it should appear." Their meetings involved Scripture reading, prayers for inspiration by the Holy Spirit, confession of the
deplorable state of humanity in general and of the lifeless state of "corrupt professors of Christianity" in particular, and pleadings for the ac-
complishment of the blessed promises associated with the coming of
Christ and the glory of the latter days. Did the united prayers of hundreds
of Christians entreating Christ to come and visit the churches constitute
proof that he was not already there? That question continued to occupy
Richard McNemar's thoughts.

During those years, McNemar also sensed a growing interest in the
end times among his frontier parishioners. In his own church many
questions were raised "concerning the reign of the Antichrist; when it
began and when it would end, and when he would appear and set up his
true kingdom." A number of people believed that this time was very near
and so "concluded it was time to leave off their vain disputes, and unite

in prayer for Christ to come and pour out his Spirit, gather his people into one, make an end of sin, and fill the earth with his glory."

FIRST APPEARANCES OF REVIVAL IN KENTUCKY

In 1798, the Presbyterian Church's General Assembly asked that a day be set aside for fasting, humiliation, and prayer to redeem the religious life of the West from "Egyptian darkness." By that time, however, renewals of pious enthusiasm had already begun in various parts of Kentucky. The most striking of these occurred under the ministry of a tall, angular Presbyterian preacher with keen black eyes and a "bold and uncompromising manner," the Reverend James McGready. Richard McNemar watched the developments with great interest.

McGready had been born in Pennsylvania of Scotch-Irish stock. His family soon moved to North Carolina and raised their son on a diet of hard work and strict Presbyterian doctrine. As a youth McGready was sent to Pennsylvania to study under the Reverend John McMillan, a graduate of the College of New Jersey. While he was there, a bout of smallpox brought McGready face to face with the question of whether or not he was prepared for eternity. He wrestled with it, and on the first Sunday after his recovery, he considered himself "converted" fully to service of the Lord.

McGready left his North Carolina parish in 1798 to manage small congregations at Red River, Gasper River, and Muddy River in Kentucky. The three churches were all located in Logan County, an area described by one frontier parson as a "Rogue's Harbor," a place abounding in desperados and other unregenerate persons.

McGready was determined to win converts in his new parish. To that end he developed a technique of impassioned preaching, diligent pastoral work, and a prayer covenant that enjoined all signers to pray every Saturday evening and Sunday morning and to devote the third Saturday of each month to prayer and fasting. All this was directed at generating a religious awakening in the community. McGready's hard work soon produced results.

In June of 1800, a "sacramental occasion" was held at Red River. The church was filled to overflowing. Presbyterian ministers William Hodge and John Rankin assisted McGready in the service. After each had spoken, a solemnity settled over the house and they stepped outside to rest. Two other pastors, Republican Methodists John and William McGee, were among the congregation, having stopped off to see for themselves the already famous McGready winning converts. According to accounts of the occasion, William McGee "felt such a power" come over him that he walked up to the pulpit, "scarcely knowing what he did," and slumped down beside it. His zeal overwhelmed him. He rose and with a trembling voice urged the congregation to submit to "the Lord Omnipotent." As he warmed up, he began to twist his way between the log benches, "shouting and exhorting with all possible energy and ecstasy."

In a moment, the floor was "covered with the slain; their screams for mercy pierced the heavens." Soon, according to McGready, one could see "profane swearers, and Sabbath-breakers pricked to the heart and crying out 'what shall we do to be saved?'"

Appraising the success that had come to the Red River communion, McGready decided to announce in advance his next sacramental meeting to be held at the Gasper River Church. Great numbers of people came in response. McGready later recalled that thirteen wagons came to transport people and provisions to the meeting.

At Gasper River there was the usual frontier dilemma: the number of worshipers exceeded the capacity of the place of worship. To remedy this situation, woodsmen cleared away the underbrush around the tiny church and built preaching stands and simple log seats. For four days the worshipers lived in makeshift tents or rested in wagons around the meeting house. Born of necessity, the "camp meeting" quickly became a part of frontier religious life.

That Sunday evening, the meetings reached a climax following a particularly vivid sermon by John McGee. Toward the end of the message the "cries of the distressed" grew in volume until they almost drowned out his voice. McGready reported that

> no person seemed to wish to go home—hunger and sleep seemed to affect nobody. Here awakening and converting work was to be found in every part of the multitude. . . . Sober professors, who had been communicants for many years, now lying prostrate on the ground, crying out in such language as this: "I have been a sober professor: I have been a communicant: . . . O! I see that religion is a sensible thing. . . . I feel the pains of hell in my soul and body! O! how I would have despised any person a few days ago, who would have acted as I am doing now! . . . But O! I cannot help it!" . . . Little children, young men and women, and old grey-bearded people, persons of every description, white and black, were to be found in every part of the multitude . . . crying out for mercy in the most extreme distress.

From the sensational successes in Logan County the revivals spread throughout Kentucky. Thousands of people flocked to the camp meetings, some attracted by the "news of these strange observations," others desiring to see for themselves this "living work of God."

CANE RIDGE—AUGUST 1801

The largest of all the Revival camp meetings was Cane Ridge. The meetings at Cane Ridge began on 6 August 1801 and continued for six days. From Friday morning to Wednesday evening the frenzied worship continued night and day without intermission. Even heavy rain failed to scatter the huge crowd, estimated at between ten to twenty-five thousand people.

The meeting began as Presbyterian, led principally by Barton Stone. However, some eighteen ministers, Presbyterian, Baptist, and Methodist, came to join in the preaching. Richard McNemar was one of them.

At 11:00 on Saturday morning two Presbyterian ministers were holding forth in the meeting house. One hundred-fifty yards away, another Presbyterian proclaimed the good news of salvation to a crowd gathered around his feet. Off in another direction a Methodist preacher had an audience closely pressed about him. Nearby was a group of black people, one of them loudly exhorting the others. Besides the preachers, small prayer groups of ten or twelve were clustered about "singing Watt's and Hart's hymns."

The young Peter Cartwright, who subsequently made great use of camp meetings, said that at times there were more than a thousand voices shouting at once, creating such a volume of noise that the sound carried for miles. James Finley, who marked his conversion from the Cane Ridge experience, described the scene:

> The noise was like the roar of Niagara. I counted seven ministers, all preaching at one time, some on stumps, others in wagons. . . . Some of the people were singing, others praying, some crying for mercy in the most piteous accents, while others were shouting most vociferously. My heart beat tumultously, my knees trembled, my lip quivered, and I felt as though I must fall to the ground. A strange supernatural power seemed to pervade the entire mass of mind there collected. . . . Soon after I left and went into the woods . . . to rally and man up my courage.
>
> After some time I returned to the scene of excitement . . . the same awfulness of feeling came over me. I stepped up on a log, where I could have a better view of the surging sea of humanity. The scene that then presented itself to my mind was indescribable. At one time I saw at least five hundred swept down in a moment, as if a battery of a thousand guns had been opened upon them, and then immediately followed shrieks and

shouts that rent the very heaven. . . . I fled for the woods a second time, and wished I had stayed at home.

A Methodist preacher, William Burke, said that under the word of God, hundreds fell prostrate on the ground before him, lay in agonies of distress, with a sinner occasionally jumping to his feet to give vent to "shouts of triumph." These McNemar took to be believers. But scoffers, too, were affected. One man, a "blasphemer," sat mounted on a horse, smiling at these unbridled religious passions, when he suddenly reeled and fell from his saddle, where he evidently remained unconscious for thirty hours. When he awoke he said he could not account for anything that had occurred during his trance. One of the most striking occurrences was that of Rachel Martin, who "was struck" on Thursday night. "She never ate nor spoke for nine days and nights. . . . Her countenance was, as it were, refined" when she finally arose.

Probably the most intense excitement at Cane Ridge was experienced on Sunday, prior to the communion service. The impassioned preaching brought about breath-taking spectacles. One preacher commented on the "one hundred persons of all classes, the learned and the unlearned, at once on the ground crying for mercy of all ages from eight to sixty years." Another reported that "undue excitement of animal feeling" resulted in at least one thousand persons being swept into the falling exercise. Soon a system of caring for the afflicted evolved. When a person was struck down, that person was carried out of the congregation. Then some minister or exhorter prayed against the background of a hymn "suitable to the occasion."

REVIVAL IN MCNEMAR'S PARISH

Late in May of 1801, a similar "extraordinary work" had broken out at Cabin Creek in northern Kentucky, where Richard McNemar was pastor.

It began on the 22nd of May, and continued four days and three nights. The scene was awful beyond description; the falling, crying out, praying, exhorting, singing, shouting . . . exhibited such new and striking evidences of a supernatural power, that few, if any, could escape without being affected. Such as tried to run from it, were frequently struck on the way, or impelled by some alarming signal to return: and so powerful was the evidence on all sides, that no place was found for the obstinate sinner to shelter himself. . . . No circumstance at this meeting appeared more striking than the great numbers that fell on the third night: and to prevent their being trodden under foot by the multitude, they were collected together and laid out in order, on two squares of the meeting-house; which, like so many dead corpses, covered a considerable part of the floor—There were persons at this meeting from Cane Ridge, Concord, Eagle Creek . . . who partook of the spirit of the work, which was a particular means of its spreading.

McNemar witnessed the "exercises" and acknowledged that excesses and immorality also accompanied the revivals. Yet in it all he was convinced that the Spirit of God was at work. Many of his Presbyterian colleagues disagreed. Some of them were convinced that a force other than God had produced the "revivals." McNemar weighed the interpretations. He considered the reactions of many colleagues as well as his own opinions.

SELECTED BIBLIOGRAPHY

Boles, John B. *The Great Revival 1787-1805: The Origins of the Southern Evangelical Mind.* Lexington: University of Kentucky Press, 1972.

Cartwright, Peter. *Autobiography of Peter Cartwright.* New York: Abingdon Press, 1956, pp. 1-108.

Johnson, Charles A. *The Frontier Camp Meeting.* Dallas: Southern Methodist University Press, 1955.

McNemar, Richard. *The Kentucky Revival.* Cincinnati: Art Guild Reprints, 1968.

Tyler, Alice Felt. *Freedom's Ferment.* New York: Harper & Row, 1962, pp. 31-46.

Weeks, Louis. *Kentucky Presbyterians.* Atlanta: John Knox Press, 1983.

Red Jacket and the Missionary Impulse

This case was prepared by Garth M. Rosell

The Reverend Mr. Cram sat speechless. The high hopes which the young missionary had brought to the Council at Buffalo Creek that hot summer morning had been nearly destroyed by the comments of Sa-Go-Ye-Wat-Ha (nicknamed Red Jacket because he regularly wore a red military jacket he had received from a British army officer), spokesperson for the chiefs and warriors of the Six Nations. Looking around the circle, he could not help but wonder if his Indian brothers and sisters would ever become part of the church of Jesus Christ. In his mind echoed the conversations that had just concluded.

INTRODUCTION BY THE AGENT OF THE UNITED STATES FOR INDIAN AFFAIRS

Brothers of the Six Nations: I rejoice to meet you at this time, and thank the Great Spirit, that he has preserved you in health, and given me another opportunity of taking you by the hand. The person who sits by me is a friend who has come a great distance to talk with you. He will inform you what his business is, and it is my request that you would listen with attention to his words.

COMMENTS BY THE MISSIONARY (THROUGH A GOVERNMENT INTERPRETER)

My friends: I am thankful for the opportunity afforded us of uniting together at this time. I had a great desire to see you and inquire into your state and welfare. For this purpose I have traveled a great distance, being sent by your old friends, the Boston Missionary Society. You will recollect they formerly sent missionaries among you to instruct you in religion and labor for your good. Although they have not heard from you for a long time, yet they have not forgotten their brothers the Six Nations, and are still anxious to do you good.

Brothers: I have not come to get your lands or your money but to enlighten your minds and to instruct you how to worship the Great Spirit agreeably to his mind and will and to preach to you the gospel of his Son, Jesus Christ. There is but one religion, and but one way to serve God, and if you do not embrace the right way, you cannot be happy hereafter. You have never worshiped the Great Spirit in a manner acceptable to him but have all your lives been in great errors and darkness. To endeavor to remove these errors and open your eyes so that you might see clearly is my business with you.

Brothers: I wish to talk with you as one friend talks with another, and if you have any objections to receive the religion which I preach, I wish you to state them, and I will endeavor to satisfy your minds and remove the objections.

Brothers: I want you to speak your minds freely, for I wish to reason with you on the subject, and if possible remove all doubts if there be any on your minds. The subject is an important one, and it is of consequence that you give it an early attention while the offer is made you. Your friends the Boston Missionary Society will continue to send you good and faithful ministers to instruct and strengthen you in religion if, on your part, you are willing to receive them.

Brothers: since I have been in this part of the country, I have visited some of your small villages and talked with your people. They appear willing to receive instructions, but, as they look up to you as their older brothers in council, they want first to know your opinion on the subject.

You have now heard what I have to propose at present. I hope you will take it into consideration and give me an answer before we part.

RED JACKET'S REPLY (FOLLOWING A TWO-HOUR CONSULTATION WITH THE CHIEFS AND WARRIORS)

Friend and brother: it was the will of the Great Spirit that we should meet together this day. He orders all things and has given us a fine day for our Council. He has taken his garment from before the sun and caused it to shine with brightness upon us. Our eyes are opened, that we see clearly; our ears are unstopped, that we have been able to hear distinctly the words you have spoken. For all these favors we thank the Great Spirit, and him only.

Brother: this council fire was kindled by you. It was at your request that we came together at this time. We have listened with attention to what you have said. You requested us to speak our minds freely. This gives us great joy, for we now consider that we stand upright before you and can speak what we think. All have heard your voice, and all speak to you now as one man. Our minds are agreed.

Brother: you say you want an answer to your talk before you leave this place. It is right you should have one, as you are a great distance from home, and we do not wish to detain you. But we will first look back a little, and tell you what our fathers have told us and what we have heard from the white people.

Brother: listen to what we say.

There was a time when our forefathers owned this great island. Their seats extended from the rising to the setting sun. The Great Spirit had made it for the use of Indians. He had created the buffalo, the deer, and other animals for food. He had made the bear and the beaver. Their skins served us for clothing. He had scattered them over the country, and taught us how to take them. He had caused the earth to produce corn for bread. All this he had done for his red children, because he loved them. If we had some disputes about our hunting ground, they were generally settled without the shedding of much blood. But an evil day came upon us. Your forefathers crossed the great water and landed on this island. Their numbers were small. They found friends and not enemies. They told us they had fled from their own country for fear of wicked men and had come here to enjoy their religion. They asked for a small seat. We took pity on them, granted their request, and they sat down amongst us. We gave them corn and meat; they gave us poison in return.

The white people had now found our country. Tidings were carried back, and more came amongst us. Yet we did not fear them. We took them to be friends. They called us brothers. We believed them and gave them a larger seat. At length their numbers had greatly increased. They wanted more land; they wanted our country. Our eyes were opened, and our minds became uneasy. Wars took place. Indians were hired to fight against Indians, and many of our people were destroyed. They also brought strong liquor amongst us. It was strong and powerful, and has slain thousands.

Brother: our seats were once large and yours were small. You have now become a great people, and we have scarcely a place left to spread our blankets. You have got our country but are not satisfied; you want to force your religion upon us.

Brother: continue to listen.

You say that you are sent to instruct us how to worship the Great Spirit agreeably to his mind, and if we do not take hold of the religion which you white people teach, we shall be unhappy hereafter. You say that you are right and we are lost. How do we know this to be true? We understand that your religion is written in a book. If it was intended for us as well as you, why has not the Great Spirit given to us—and not only to us, but why did he not give to our forefathers the knowledge of that book with the means of understanding it rightly? We only know what you tell us about it. How shall we know when to believe, being so often deceived by the white people?

Brothers: you say there is but one way to worship and serve the Great Spirit. If there is but one religion, why do you white people differ so much about it? Why not all agreed, as you can all read the book?

Brother: we do not understand these things.

We are told that your religion was given to your forefathers and has been handed down from father to son. We also have a religion which was given to our forefathers and has been handed down to us their children. We worship in that way. It teaches us to be thankful for all the favors we receive, to love each other and to be united. We never quarrel about religion.

Brother: the Great Spirit has made us all, but he has made a great difference between his white and red children. He has given us different complexions and different customs. To you he has given the arts. To these he has not opened our eyes. We know these things to be true. Since he has made so great a difference between us in other things, why may we not conclude that he has given us a different religion according to our understanding? The Great Spirit does right. He knows what is best for his children; we are satisfied.

Brother: we do not wish to destroy your religion or take it from you. We only want to enjoy our own.

Brother: we are told that you have been preaching to the white people in this place. These people are our neighbors. We are acquainted with them. We will wait a little while and see what effect your preaching has upon them. If we find it does them good, makes them honest and less disposed to cheat Indians, we will then consider again of what you have said.

Brother: you have now heard our answer to your talk, and this is all we have to say at present.

As we are going to part, we will come and take you by the hand and hope the Great Spirit will protect you on your journey and return you safe to your friends.

AFTERMATH

The young missionary was both confused and troubled by what he had just heard. Unable fully to collect his thoughts, he rose quickly as Red Jacket and the others approached him with their hands outstretched. Almost before he knew it, he had refused to shake their hands—able only to comment quietly through the interpreter something about the fact that there should be no fellowship between "the religion of God and the works of the devil."

Yet as he turned to leave, Cram wondered if he had done the right thing. Red Jacket had raised some fundamental questions. "Will I ever be able to overcome their objections?" he thought to himself. "Will these people ever become part of the church of Jesus Christ?"

SELECTED BIBLIOGRAPHY

Beaver, Robert Pierce. *Church, State, and the American Indians: Two and a Half Centuries of Partnership in Mission between Protestant Churches and Government.* St. Louis: Concordia, 1966.

Bemis, James D., ed. *Indian Speeches Delivered by Farmer's Brother and Red Jacket, Two Seneca Chiefs.* N.p., 1809.

Stone, William L. *The Life and Times of Red Jacket, or Sa-Go-Ye-Wat-Ha, being the sequel to the History of the Six Nations.* 1841; rpt., St. Clair Shores, Mich.: Scholarly Press, 1970.

Underhill, Ruth Murray. *Red Man's Religion: Beliefs and Practices of the Indian North of Mexico.* Chicago: University of Chicago Press, 1965.

Vanderwerth, W. C. *Indian Oratory: Famous Speeches by Noted Indian Chieftains.* Norman: University of Oklahoma Press, 1971.

Washburn, Wilcomb E., ed. *The Indian and the White Man.* New York: New York University Press, 1964.

Lyman Beecher: Calvinist Orthodoxy and the New Theology

This case was prepared by Louis B. Weeks

"Dr. Wilson, this is the third time you have misrepresented me, and I shall correct you until you put it right." Lyman Beecher, seated in a pulpit chair in his own Second Presbyterian Church, Cincinnati, stared directly at his accuser Dr. Joshua Wilson, minister of the city's First Presbyterian Church. Beecher faced a friendly climate, but a serious charge—heresy in the Reformed doctrines he taught and preached.

THE BIG GUN OF CALVINISM

Born in New Haven, Connecticut, in October 1775, Lyman Beecher gravitated naturally to Yale when he wished to study for the ministry. There he was increasingly appalled at the rationalism rampant among his fellow students and increasingly sympathetic with the steps the new president, Timothy Dwight, was taking to increase the measure of Christian belief among them. Upon graduation from Yale in 1797, Beecher undertook ministry at East Hampton on Long Island, where he sought to augment the efforts of other Christian pastors promoting discipleship to Christ and inveighing against religious infidelity.

> I did not attack infidelity directly. Not at all. That would have been cracking the whip behind a runaway team—made them run the faster. I always preached right to the conscience. Every sermon with my eye on the gun to hit somebody. Went through the doctrines; showed what they didn't mean; what they did; then argument; knocked away objections, and drove home on the conscience. . . . At first there was winking and blinking from below the gallery, forty or fifty exchanging glances, smiling, and watching. But when that was over, infidelity was ended.

Beecher's efforts to bring a real revival of religious vitality to the congregation and to the community at East Hampton met with mixed results at best. His subsequent pastorate in Litchfield afforded much the same outcome, although Beecher had by now gained a reputation as both preacher and Calvinist reformer. He was called to Boston as "the big gun of Calvinism" to combat the rank heresy so appealingly propounded by a growing number of sophisticated Unitarians. In 1826 the Beecher family moved to the "Hub of the Universe" (as Boston was then described), and old "brimstone Beecher" (as his critics named him) went to work. He sought to foster a "continuous revival" and to battle rationalism, Boston's rum houses, and the influence of the large numbers of Roman Catholic immigrants arriving at that time.

Of course Beecher's theology was not unaffected by his reform endeavors, his millennial hopes, and the American scene in general. He grew to listen more to another theologian, Nathanial Taylor, who accentuated human ability and the possibility of reform. Beecher followed Taylor in coming to understand God more in terms of his benevolence than of his arbitrary justice. People, in this scheme of things, were personally responsible for their own guilt (in the Fall), moral agents free to respond to God's offer of grace. "Man found the benefit of the atonement within easier reach than formerly; and grace, now resistible, was in greater supply."

THE NEW THEOLOGY

Beecher surprised adherents and opponents alike when he announced in 1832 that he would accept the presidency of the nascent Lane Theological Seminary in Cincinnati, Ohio. Among those evidently most stunned by the news was the Presbyterian minister Joshua Lacy Wilson, who had concurred in offering Lyman the invitation. Wilson, who had arrived in Cincinnati in 1808 and had been shepherd of the First Presbyterian Church there ever since, served on Lane's board. There would seem to have been a number of things that eventuated in a deteriorioation of the personal relationship between Wilson and Beecher. Wilson may have been jealous of Beecher when the latter was called to serve concurrently as pastor of the rival Second Presbyterian Church, disappointed that Beecher accepted a call he wanted himself. At any rate, in time he instituted proceedings to exclude Beecher from the Presbytery, bringing charges of heresy against him.

Wilson specifically charged Beecher with having espoused "deviations" made from the Westminster Standards. Wilson was a member of the Old School of American Presbyterianism, which loved the Westminster Confession of Faith "covers and all." The insistences on Beecher's part that "man had some ability," that God was so good that he might not be God (as they read and heard New School thought), and that "revival" was possible all met with serious problems when compared with the Standards. The actual charges against Beecher were made 9 June 1835 before Cincinnati Presbytery, as follows:

I. I charge Dr. Beecher with propogating doctrines contrary to the word of God, and the standards of the Presbyterian church, on the subject of the depraved nature of man.

II. I charge Dr. Beecher with propogating doctrines contrary to the word of God, and the standards of the Presbyterian church, on the subject of Total Depravity and the work of the Holy Spirit in effectual calling.

III. I charge Dr. Beecher with propogating a doctrine of perfection contrary to the standards of the Presbyterian churches.

IV. I charge Dr. Beecher with the sin of slander (for teaching doctrines contrary to church standards and misrepresenting the standards).

V. I charge Dr. Beecher with the crime of preaching the same, and kindred doctrines, contained in these sermons, in the Second Presbyterian Church, in Cincinnati.

VI. I charge Dr. Beecher with the sin of hypocrisy; I mean dissimulation, in important religious matters.

Beecher admitted that he preached and taught that people are responsible and free agents in choosing to be dependent in light of God's providence. He strongly denied any measure of hypocrisy in upholding human ability on the one hand and God's predestining activity on the other. Rather, he maintained, the Bible, and John Calvin too, upheld both election and human responsibility. Thus he pleaded Not Guilty to the charges as Wilson set them forth.

Wilson asked Beecher if indeed in subscribing to the Westminster Standards he did not imply that they contained the "truth, the whole truth, and nothing but the truth"? If he did subscribe to them in such a thoroughgoing manner, then it was heretical to preach and teach doctrines obviously contrary to their "plain" meaning.

Beecher contended that Wilson was exercising presumption unbecoming a Christian when he sought to contain God's ways of working in some metaphysical speculation. He acknowledged that there are rules and agreements held in common among members of a voluntary association, even a religious communion. Wilson, though, was accusing him of heresy "according to the plain and obvious meaning" of the Standards. "Your 'plain and obvious meaning' is not my 'plain and obvious meaning,'" he said.

In the trial, which lasted for a whole week, Beecher repeatedly asserted that "the language never stands still," that Calvin represented essentially the same theology that "New School" Presbyterianism now sought to manifest, and that the Bible supported every one of his alleged heresies. Wilson countered that Beecher knew that in accenting human ability he participated in both Pelagian and Arminian heresies, anathema to Calvinism and the Standards.

Exhibit I

Excerpts from "Dependence and Free Agency," a Sermon by Lyman Beecher

One of the Chief Documents Employed by Dr. Joshua Wilson to Substantiate His Charges of Heresy against Dr. Beecher

"Without me ye can do nothing."
—John 15:5

It is manifest, from the Bible, that Jesus Christ is the acting Divinity of the universe. Everywhere the attributes, works, and worship, which belong to God, are ascribed to him. Omniscience, omnipresence, omnipotence, eternity, immutability, infinite benevolence, justice, mercy and truth, are his attributes; and his works and such as correspond with them. He made all things, and by him all things consist. It is he who in the beginning said, "Let there be light, and there was light"; who is revealed as "upholding all things by the word of his power"; who governs material agents, and sways the sceptre of moral empire over earth and heaven. The law is in his hand as Mediator, and the Gospel with its remedial influence; and he is "head over all things to the church." It was his praise which the morning stars "sang together," and which animated the heavenly host when they shouted, "Glory to God in the highest, and on earth peace, good will toward men."

The text announces the universal and entire dominion of Jesus Christ, and the universal and entire dependence of man upon him for ability to do anything. This dependence, like the nature of his government, is of two kinds, natural and moral. The one is occasioned by our incapacity of self-existence, and self-sustained physical action. The other is a dependence resulting from our sinful character, and the consequent necessity of an atonement and a moral renovation to secure our pardon and meetness for heaven.

I propose, in this discourse, to give a scriptural account of the dependence of man upon Jesus Christ, in both these respects; as a creature and as a sinner.

As a creature, it is obvious that man is dependent on Christ for all his natural and moral powers. In his material organization, it was Christ that "did see his substance yet being unperfect, and in whose book all his members were written, which in continuance were fashioned, when as yet there was none of them." It was Christ who created his mind, his power of thought, and of mental and moral action; his perception, judgment, reason; his capacity of happiness and misery; his ability—under the guidance and influence of the government of God—to choose the good and refuse the evil. These are all attributes given him in creation, and from the constitution according to which his being will be continued. . . .

This dependence upon Christ for successful effort extends to the intellectual as well as to the physical nature of man. Through the medium of disease, he can send upon the mind bewildered thoughts, impaired memory, incapacity of attention, instability of purpose, and fear and faintness of heart. Upon the ordering of his Providence depend, also, not only our capacities, but all our opportunities for successful action. All have not been Luthers, or Bonapartes, who may have possessed the capacity of acting the part which they acted. He who creates the endowments of man puts them into ample requisition, or sends them into relative obscurity. Nor is it in the power of human greatness, even with opportunity, to secure the successful execution of the wisest plans; for this depends on innumerable contingencies, unforeseen to any but the eye of God; upon natural causes, unmanageable by human power; and upon human volitions, affected by the innumerable motives included in the ever-varying Providence of God; and on the passions and prejudices and conflicting interests of men. Nothing is more impenetrable than the veil which hides from man those events of futurity which depend on human volitions and actions.

Such is the dependence of man upon Christ as a creature. But there is another kind of dependence, resulting from his character and condition as a sinner. This condition is hopeless, without Christ. Direct forgiveness of sin, on condition of repentance, is impossible, upon principles of law. To make an atonement, was what man could not do; and to save without an atonement, was "what the law could not do." The influence of law depends on its rewards and its penalties. Suspend these, and you paralyze its power, and in the same degree you impair its influence upon the mind, and open the door to rebellion and anarchy.

For that influence, therefore, which sustains the law of God, and opens the door of mercy to a lost world, men are dependent on the Lord Jesus Christ. The law could not forgive and maintain its power. Angels could make no atonement, and no man could redeem his brother. Works could not justify, and the blood of bulls and of goats, and the ashes of an heifer, could not take away sin. Thousands of rams, and of rivers of oil, and the blood of the first-born, could not purchase redemption. The inability of man to make an atonement for sin was therefore a natural impossibility, absolute and entire. . . .

The sinner can be accountable, then and he is accountable, for his impenitence and unbelief, though he will not turn, and God may never turn him, because he is able and only unwilling to do what God commands, and which, being done, would save his soul. Indeed, to be able and unwilling to obey God, is the only possible way in which a free agent can become deserving of condemnation and punishment. So long as he is able and willing to obey there can be no sin; and the moment the ability of obedience ceases, the commission of sin becomes impossible. . . .

And the more clear the light of his conviction shines, the more distinct is the sinner's perception that he is, not destitute of capacity, but inflexibly unwilling to obey the Gospel. Does the Spirit of God produce convictions which are contrary to fact, and contrary to the teaching of the Bible? Never. What, then, when he moves on to that work of sovereign mercy, which no sinner ever resisted, and without which no one ever submitted to God—what does he do? When he pours the daylight of omniscience upon the soul, and comes to search out what is amiss, and put in order that which is out of the way, what impediment to obedience does he find to be removed, and what work does he perform? He finds only the will perverted, and obstinately persisting in its sinful choice; and in the day of his power all he accomplishes is, to make the sinner willing.

It is not grace resisted alone, but the ability of man perverted and abused, that brings down upon him guilt and condemnation. The influence of the Spirit belongs wholly to the remedial system. Whereas ability commensurate with requirement is the equitable and everlasting foundation of the moral government of God.

The facts in the case are just the other way. The doctrine of man's free agency and natural ability as the ground of obligation and guilt, and of his impotency of will by reason of sin, has been the received doctrine of the orthodox church in all ages.

Both doctrines are true, and exist in perfect harmony; and by their united action, bring on the mind a strength of obligation, and weight of guilt, and a power of motive, wholly unparalleled by any other mode of exhibiting the Gospel which I have ever known. It has been said that they ought never to be preached together in the same sermon. It would be nearer the truth to say that they ought never to be separated. Should free agency and ability be so preached as to make and justify the impression that man is so able and so willing to obey the Gospel as that the special influence of the Spirit is not necessary to make him actually willing, it would be a doctrine fundamentally erroneous; and were dependence so preached as to make and justify the impression that God requires of men the performance of natural impossibilities, and that all which a sinner can do is impenitently to use the means and wait for sovereign grace;—this would be the subversion of accountability, and of all the principles of the moral government of God. It is when the capacity of man for obedience is asserted, and his own perversion of it is charged upon him, and God commands him to repent, and Christ, who died for him, exhorts, and his ambassadors plead, and the Spirit strives; that the commandment comes, and fear is awakened, and conscience armed, and sin revives, and the sinner dies. Experience evinces continually, in revivals, that there is no pressure upon the soul like that which is produced by the recognition of ability self-perverted, and the necessity of special divine influence self-created, by inflexible obstinacy in sin. If there be any truth which ever brought this soul of mine into the dust before God, with a conscious guilt which was insupportable, and an anguish the recollection of which the sages of eternity cannot obliterate; it was the distinct perception of immortal powers voluntarily withdrawn from the service of God, and the' certainty of a profitless and miserable eternity, if in the day of his power he did not make me willing to obey him. Day after day, and month after month, amid darkness visible and sickness of heart from hope deferred, this was the iron that entered my soul, and drew fast upon me the bands of death,—that God had made me capable of his perfect, blessed, immortal sevice, and I had turned away from it to beggarly elements; that by the blood of expiation he had opened to me a door of return, while my own obstinacy and God's justice threatened me with an eternity of everlasting uselessness, and guilt, and misery. And it was here, if anywhere, that God, by his truth, broke my hard heart and bowed my stubborn will.

And I must say, that while such has been my own experience of the two doctrines upon my own soul, such, also, during my whole ministry, has been my observation of their effects on the souls of others. They have constituted, under God, the power of my ministry, the burning focus and the breaking hammer; and so vital are the two principles and so interwoven and diffused in all those discourses of mine which God has made most effectual in the conviction and conversion of sinners, that I could not preach one of them in a revival, after these principles had been obliterated. No other obstruction to the success of the Gospel is so great as the possession of the public mind by the belief of the natural and absolute inability of unconverted men. That belief has done more, I verily believe, to wrap in sackcloth the Sun of Righteousness, and perpetuate the shadow of death on those who might have been rejoicing in his light, than all errors beside. I cannot anticipate a greater calamity to the church than would follow its universal inculcation and adoption. And most blessed and glorious, I am confident, will be the result, when her ministry, everywhere, shall rightly understand and teach, and their hearers universally shall admit, that the full ability of every sinner to comply with the terms of salvation, and the voluntary and obstinate perversion of this ability, together constitute the ground of the indispensableness of converting grace. So preached Apostles and Reformers and other successful ambassadors for Christ; and so was their message received by the multitudes in whom it was made the power of God unto salvation. And so will ministers universally preach, and their message be received, when all kindreds, and people, and tongues, shall be subdued to the obedience of faith.

SELECTED BIBLIOGRAPHY

Beecher, Charles, ed. *Autobiography, Correspondence, Etc. of Lyman Beecher, D.D.* 2 Vols. New York: Harper, 1865.

Beecher, Lyman. *The Autobiography of Lyman Beecher.* Edited by Barbara Cross. 2 Vols. Cambridge: Belknap Press, 1961.

Henry, Stuart. *Unvanquished Puritan: A Portrait of Lyman Beecher.* Grand Rapids: Eerdmans, 1973.

McLoughlin, William G. *Modern Revivalism: Charles Grandison Finney to Billy Graham.* New York: Ronald Press, 1959.

Wood, Raymond L. "Lyman Beecher, 1775-1863: A Biographical Study." Ph.D. dissertation, Yale University, 1961.

Asahel Nettleton and the Emergence of the Finney Revivals

This case was prepared by Garth M. Rosell

By the time the Convention got underway on the 18th of July 1827, the Reverend Mr. Asahel Nettleton knew he had a fight on his hands. The eighteen Congregational and Presbyterian ministers who had gathered in the little New York village of New Lebanon, including many of the most influential church leaders in New England, were deeply divided over the crisis that had been brewing in their churches for over two years. While all agreed that religious revivals were essential to the life and growth of the church, the delegates disagreed strongly about the kinds of measures appropriate to their promotion. A convention had been called to decide on the matter.

ASAHEL NETTLETON

Since his graduation from Yale College and subsequent ordination in the Congregational Church, Nettleton had pursued his career as an itinerant evangelist. Traveling from town to town throughout New England, he sought to aid local ministers in the promotion of orderly and dignified revivals within their parishes. Although his activities had been greatly curtailed following his contraction of typhus in 1822, from which he never fully recovered, he continued to maintain a lively interest in anything having to do with religious revivals. Indeed, he considered himself in many ways to be the successor of his favorite teacher at Yale, President Timothy Dwight (who had died in 1817), as the leader of the revival forces in the East. Many of his Congregational colleagues concurred in that judgment. Lyman Beecher, pastor of Boston's Hanover Street Church, for example, virtually placed Nettleton in a class by himself.

Comparing him with another well-known preacher of the day, Beecher commented that he considered Nettleton ''as far above him in talent, wisdom, judgment, and experience, as Bonaparte was removed from one of the corporals in the French Army.''

Revivals were important to the strategies of Nettleton and Beecher. Both used revivals to battle religious infidelity as well as to secure new members for the churches. They sought diligently, therefore, to protect revivals from the kinds of abuses and excesses they believed had damaged them in the past. Viewing themselves as the ''Watchmen of the East,'' as Nettleton put it, they established strict guidelines for the practice of revivals. These procedures, which Beecher later labeled ''old measures,'' included such safeguards as (1) establishing a period of ''probation,'' from two months to a year, between conversion and full membership in the church; (2) guarding vigorously against excessive emotional outbreaks in public worship; (3) strictly limiting the number of special preaching and prayer services to be held in any given week; (4) avoiding the use of colloquial or abusive language in sermons and prayers; and (5) making sure that women were not allowed to pray in mixed assemblies. ''If revival efforts are embarrassed'' and ''religion is disgraced and trodden down,'' Beecher told his friend Asahel, the work of God would be greatly damaged. ''There are some things which adorn, and some that disgrace religion.'' If revivalists ''strip religion of the mildness, and kindness, and courtesy of civilized decorum, and exhibit her in alliance with all the repellences and roughnesses of uncultivated humanity,'' he warned, they will reduce our Christian nation to the level of savage ones. Both Beecher and Nettleton were convinced that revival should be conducted in good taste.

THE WESTERN REVIVALS

Nettleton received with interest reports of new revival activity in central and western New York State when they began to filter over the mountains into New England late in 1825. Settled largely by people of New England stock, central and western New York had experienced revivals before. Indeed, the fires of revival had so persistently swept over that area that it became known in popular language as the ''burned-over district.'' These new ''Western revivals,'' however, had a different quality. Headed by a charismatic young lawyer, Charles G. Finney, they seemed to be spreading more rapidly and exhibiting more vitality than anything the settlements had seen for a long time.

Most of the revival activity was centered in the major Presbyterian Churches of Oneida County: the Reverend Mr. Nathan S. S. Beman's Presbyterian Church of Troy, the Reverend Mr. Samuel C. Aiken's Presbyterian Church of Utica, the Reverend Mr. John Frost's Presbyterian Church of Whitesboro, and the Reverend Mr. Noah Coe's Presbyterian Church of New Hartford, to mention a few. Indeed, the Presbyterians dominated the religious life of the entire region. Theoretically, of course, the 1801 Plan of Union had merged Presbyterians with Congregationalists, at least for purposes of missionary strategy. In Oneida County, however, several Congregational ministers, disenchanted with the arrangement, had pulled out of the Oneida Presbytery and revived the Congregational Oneida Association. Led by the Reverend Mr. William Weeks, minister of the Congregational Church in Paris Hill, New York, and a good friend of Nettleton, the Oneida Association ministers launched an all-out attack upon the revivals.

Charging Finney and his Presbyterian colleagues with using unscriptural and inappropriate "new measures" such as the hasty granting of church membership to revival converts, the tendency to allow the feelings to control the judgment, the use of "protracted" meetings (holding services on a series of successive evenings), the employment of colloquial or abusive language in sermons and prayers, and the practice of allowing women to pray in mixed assemblies, the Oneida Association ministers systematically wrote letters, printed articles, and preached sermons aimed at ending the revival impetus.

Local Unitarians and Universalists likewise sought to discredit the movement. Labeling Finney the "madman of Oneida" and his preaching as rhetoric best "suited to a Bacchanalian row," they accused him of terrifying "weak-minded women and children half out of their senses with his descriptions of hell and his imagery of the infernal regions, with which," they concluded, "he seems to be quite familiar." One man even wrote his nephew a letter warning him about Finney and asking him to stay away from the meetings: "William, beware," he wrote, "beware . . . this noted Finney's character it is said to be verry bad (I know nothing personally). I have been informed that he was bred a lawyer and has had two wives without loosing any and has had a child born to him by a third female since he was married. . . . William," he pled, "look well at the foundation. Strip this man of his briefs and perseverance and what is he?"

Such wild reports, with little or no evidence given in support, troubled Nettleton. Especially disturbing were the letters from his friend Weeks. As "Watchman of the East," he felt it was his job to curb such excesses, lest his own revivals be damaged by association. Furthermore, he was disturbed by such charges as those made by the editor of the *Evangelical Magazine,* who claimed Finney to be saying in effect, "Brother Nettleton, you've been Captain long enough; 'tis my turn now." Indeed, by early January of 1827, Nettleton felt he had heard enough. Consequently, on January 13 he wrote a long letter to the Reverend Mr. Samuel Aiken, whose church in Utica was the scene of one of Finney's most notable revivals. He expressed his concern over the direction the "Western Revivals" were taking. Later that month, Beecher wrote a similar letter to the Reverend Mr. Nathan S. S. Beman in Troy. While the Yale men expressed joy at the arrival of revival in the West, both decried the widespread and inappropriate use of the "new measures," which they believed would be ruinous in their consequences. "There has doubtless been a work of grace in Troy," Nettleton admitted to Aiken, "but it has been at an awful expense." Indeed, he continued, "many young men" in the West "are continually violating the rules of ministerial order and Christian propriety. . . . Impatient to see the temple rise, they are now doing that, which, it appears to me, will tend ultimately, more than anything else, to defeat the end which they wish to accomplish." In short, "they are . . . pulling down in many places, the very things which I have been helping ministers to build up."

Aiken and Beman, in their responses to the Yale brethren, expressed appreciation for the interest and concern their New England colleagues were expressing in their letters. Yet, as Nettleton was fully aware, they were more than a little peeved at what they felt were inaccuracies and unkindnesses in the charges that had been laid to their account. Nettleton knew that since September 1826, three members of the Oneida Presbytery—John Frost, Moses Gillet, and Noah Coe—had been gathering reports on the revivals for the purpose of publishing an official Presbytery narrative of the movement. The three ministers had also been commissioned by Prebytery to address themselves particularly to the charges that had been leveled against the revivals. Their findings did not please Nettleton. The *Narrative of the Revival of Religion in the County of Oneida,* published in April of 1827, maintained a position strongly supportive of the "Western Revivals." Pointing out that many of the rumors about revival excesses were little more than erroneous fabrications by enemies and strongly supporting the appropriateness and effectiveness of the "new measures," the report concluded, "God has made a rich and wonderful display of his grace amongst us during the past year, in the conversion of sinners, and the quickening of his children. More than three thousand are indulging hope that they have become reconciled to

God through the Redeemer. . . . Never before have the churches in this region been blessed with so great a shower of divine grace.''

THE NEW LEBANON CONVENTION

As the buds of spring began to arrive in 1827, it was becoming clear to Nettleton that a crisis had arisen in the church that would not pass quickly. Although he did not initiate the idea of gathering all the interested parties together in a convention to work out the problem, he agreed to it when Beecher proposed it to him. Beecher and Beman had worked out the details of the gathering for the purpose of seeing ''in what respect there is an agreement between brethren from different sections of the country, in regard to principles and measures in conducting the promoting of revivals of religion.'' The convention was set to meet in New Lebanon from the 18th to the 21st of July 1827. Invitations were sent out to the leading ministers of the Northeast.

Eighteen prominent Congregational and Presbyterian clergymen indicated that they planned to attend: Justin Edwards, minister of the Congregational Church at Andover Seminary; Heman Humphrey, president of Amherst College; Lyman Beecher, minister of the Hanover Street Church in Boston; Caleb Tenney and Joel Hawes, both ministers of Congregational churches in Connecticut; Silas Churchill, host for the convention and minister of the Congregational Church in New Lebanon; Norton and Wed, Henry Smith and Dirck Lansing, ministers from New York: George Gale, minister of the Presbyterian Church in Western, New York, and later founder of Knox College in Galesburg, Illinois; as well as Asahel Nettleton, Nathan S. S.Beman, William R. Weeks, Moses Gillet, John Frost, Samuel Aiken, and Charles Finney.

The delegates were divided over the ''new measures'' question, each holding his own position as to the appropriateness or inappropriateness of the new procedures for use in promoting revivals. There was particularly deep division over the question of whether or not women should be allowed to pray in ''promiscuous assemblies,'' as they put it. Yet underlying the divisions, as Nettleton and his New England colleagues became increasingly aware, was an essential unity on many substantial questions. Resolution after resolution was adopted without a dissenting vote. Some of the ''Eastern'' brethren had expected to see a collection of ''wild-eyed fanatics'' and ''madmen'' confronting them at meetings. ''We crossed the mountains,'' Beecher commented, ''expecting to meet a company of boys, but we found them to be full-grown men.'' Furthermore, the New

Englanders discovered that many of the reports they had heard of wild goings-on in the meetings simply were not true. While there were real differences, to be sure, there was little question that Finney and his followers gained considerable stature during those days together.

Nettleton, however, began to feel betrayed. What he hoped would be a forum in which a needed lesson might be taught to the young and inexperienced revivalists from the West and by which they might be brought gently but firmly under the experienced and benevolent oversight of the "Watchmen of the East" seemed to be turning rather into an occasion of capitulation to the leadership of Charles Finney and the adoption of the "new measures." Visibly agitated by the course of the meetings, Nettleton frequently had to leave the sessions to walk through the village or retire to his room. Exhausted and bewildered, he wondered what sort of strategy he should adopt since his first plan seemed to be failing. Should he resist these strange turns of events or surrender to them?

Exhibit I

Excerpt from the *Narrative of the Revival of Religion in the County of Oneida*

1. From the preceding accounts, we are constrained to acknowledge that God has made a rich and wonderful display of his grace amongst us during the past year, in the conversion of sinners, and the quickening of his children. *More than three thousand* are indulging hope that they have become reconciled to God through the Redeemer. About half this number have already united with the Presbyterian and Congregational churches, and a large portion of the remainder with the Baptist and Methodist churches. Never before have the churches in this region been blessed with so great a shower of divine grace.

2. This revival has continued longer, particularly in some of our societies, than has been usual in former revivals. It is now more than a year since it commenced in some places where it still continues; and in most of our churches, an unusual spirit of prayer still prevails, and instances of conviction and conversion continue to occur.

3. Considering the number of converts, and the time that has elapsed since the revival commenced, the instances of backsliding have been fewer than usual. From the preceding narrative, it appears, that, with few exceptions, those who have indulged hope, are steadfast, and growing in knowledge and grace. By their fruits in future life their real character must be tested.

4. In this revival there has been less appearance of mere sympathy and excitement of the passions, unaccompanied with *conviction of sin,* than usual. Most of the feeling, and the strongest feeling, which sinners have manifested, has arisen from the lashes of an accusing conscience. So far as this

characteristic of the revival is owing to means, we believe it has been to the fact, that Christians have prayed much for the convicting and sanctifying influence of the Spirit, and that ministers have constantly pressed the consciences of sinners with those truths which show them their guilt, and their immediate duty to repent and believe. The whole man has been addressed— his understanding, his conscience, and his affections. The general strain of preaching has been far from what is usually denominated *declamatory;* and it has been equally far from what is styled, by the gay, the flippant, and the superficial part of community, *oratorical* and *popular.* There is a style of preaching, under which such hearers will *feel strongly,* and *love* to *feel;* and under which they may even weep, as they would over a favorite novel; and from which they will retire, delighted with the powers of the speaker, and the beauties of his composition. But such is not the preaching, under which sinners have been pricked in their hearts, and led to cry out—"Men and brethren, what shall we do?"

5. This revival has been characterized by a remarkable spirit of prayer. Often has it been said—"Christians pray as they have never prayed before." Many have been in deep distress, and felt what it was to *travail* in *birth* for souls. With this burden pressing upon their hearts, they have cried to God for help, feeling they could not let him go without a blessing; and where Christians have been united and persevering in their supplications, astonishing, and in some instances, overwhelming influences of the Spirit have been witnessed. So great, and so general has been the excitement, that worldly business was in a considerable degree suspended, and religion was the common topic of conversation in all companies and in all places.

6. Unusual strength of faith in the promises and threatenings of God has been manifested in many of our churches. Christians have not only assented to the testimony of God, that there is a heaven and a hell; but they have seemed, in many instances, to have such a spiritual perception of these amazing truths, and others connected with them, that they have *rejoiced with trembling.*

7. An unusual spirit of prayer has prevailed among converts, and they have manifested a disposition to converse with their friends and others on the subject of religion. It has often been remarked of them, that they were born praying. Many of them appear to have the strength of spiritual manhood, and promise to be among the brightest ornaments of our churches.

8. This revival has extended to all classes of society. Some have been born again in *old* age. Many, very young, have given satisfactory evidence of piety, especially among those who have been trained in religious families, and in our Sabbath schools. Many men of wealth, and learning, and talents, have been converted, and become like little children. Many, who in common parlance were moral men, have seen that their morality was devoid of that holiness of heart, "without which no man shall see the Lord," and have cried, "God be merciful to me a sinner." Many, who had embraced universalism and other errors, have fled from their refuges of *lies,* to lay hold of the

hope set before them in the gospel. These facts should encourage ministers and churches to pray and labour for the salvation of *all men,* the high and the low, the rich and the poor, the old and the young, the moral and the profane, animated with the thought that ''he that converteth a sinner from the error of his ways, shall save a soul from death, and hide a multitude of sins.''

9. Great heart-searchings among professors have characterized this revival. This we have seen in former revivals, but never before to so great an extent. It has been very common to hear professors say, with a solemn, downcast countenance, ''I have no religion.'' They have had severe seasons of conviction. Some probably have, for the first time, been brought to repentance. Most, however, have, after a short time, given evidence of an increased devotion to God; and such have been eminently useful in promoting the work. Those ministers, also, in whose societies the revival has been powerful, have been led to close self-examination, and been apparently deeply humbled for past unfaithfulness.

10. Converts, especially during the greatest excitement, have manifested more joy and stronger hopes, than in any preceding revivals among us. Strong hopes have been considered by many an unfavourable indication. Whether this be a correct opinion, we shall not undertake to determine. But it is worthy of consideration, whether the faint hopes of converts may not arise from not being earnestly pressed with truths adapted to their case, and from the want of more spiritual strength in the church, in wrestling with God in prayer for their deliverance from sin, rather than from deep humility, and a just sense of danger of deception.

11. Much opposition has been made to this revival. This appears from the preceding accounts. But the half is not told, and for the honour of the county, we think, ought not to be told. False reports have been circulated. Gross misrepresentations have been made of the preaching, and other means which have been employed to promote the work. Prejudices have thus been excited in the minds of some, who are doubtless the friends of religion, but who have not been in circumstances favourable to judge for themselves. It is not to be expected, that men actuated by the best motives, and pursuing with hallowed zeal the most noble objects, should act with perfect wisdom and discretion. But from the preceding accounts, and from personal observation, the committee feel warranted in saying, that ministers and churches have exhibited as much sound wisdom and discretion, as has ever been exhibited in any revival of which they have any knowledge. Yea, we believe that there has been an unusual spirit of prayer to God, for the wisdom which is profitable to direct.

It would savour of weakness and spiritual pride in our churches, to justify every thing which has been said and done, in public and private, by the friends of the revival. But we believe it a duty we owe to the cause of truth, to say, that most of the opposition has been excited by that preaching, and those means, which have met the approbation of the great Head of the Church. Indiscretions, real or apparent, are the only things which have given most of the opposers any *pleasure*. Their consciences, could they speak, would tell the world, that ninety-nine hundredths of all the *stir* they have made, has originated from a naked exhibition of gospel truth, and from the agonizing prayers and faithful exertions of the people of God for the salvation of their fellow-man.

It is not the wish of the committee to dwell upon this opposition. Care has been taken to guard the churches from talking much about the opposition, and allowing their personal feelings to become enlisted by the falsehood and abuse of opposers. But we have said thus much, to give the Christian public what we verily believe a just representation of this outcry, and to prevent any from being alarmed at opposition to revivals, and neglecting to use means which God blesses in promoting them. We believe, from the history of the church, and facts that have occurred in this revival strengthen the belief, that the elements of opposition to a revival of "pure and undefiled religion," exist in the most enlightened and moral districts of christendom, and are to be found in that pride, and worldliness, and ambition, and love of pleasure, which reign predominant in the heart of the unrenewed, and which exist to an alarming extent among ministers, elders, deacons, and private members of the church of Christ. Many, in Christian as well as heathen lands, have their idols, and they are too strongly attached to them to give up without a severe struggle. Those who would attempt the work, must count the cost, and make up their minds to put on the whole Christian armour, and prepare to receive many fiery darts from the enemy, before he will submit.

Means Which Appear to Have Been Blessed in Promoting This Revival

1. Seasons of fasting and prayer. In most, if not all, the societies which have shared in this work of grace, days have been set apart for the special object of praying for the influences of the Spirit, to humble and sanctify the professed disciples of Christ, and to convert sinners.

2. Confession of sin in churches. Wherever churches have met, and with evident *sincerity* of *heart,* confessed their "faults one to another," God has granted them a sweet sense of his forgiving mercy, given them free access to his throne of grace in praying for others, and great boldness and zeal in using means for their salvation.

3. Church discipline. This has tended to humble churches, and to alarm the impenitent. Discipline, judiciously administered, has been found a powerful method of enforcing some of the truths of the gospel.

4. Visiting from house to house. This has been done extensively. These visits have been strictly religious. Every member of the family, capable of receiving instruction, has been addressed; and such visits have usually been closed with prayer, adapted to the character and circumstances of the different members of the family. By such visits, many have been addressed who could be addressed no where else, and who were thus brought to attend on the usual means of grace; cold professors have been roused, and many careless sinners awakened.

5. Preaching the gospel, its doctrines and precepts, its promises and threatenings, with *great plainness* and *earnestness*. Every class of people have been addressed with truths adapted to their character—Churches have been reproved in the most pointed manner, for their lukewarmness, their pride, and worldiness, and unbelief. They have been urged as strongly to repent and humble themselves before God, as the most rebellious sinners. This plain and faithful application of divine truth to the churches, while it has produced great searchings of heart, and led some to abandon their hopes, has in several cases, excited greater alarm among sinners than a direct address. The truths of God's Word have been pressed upon sinners without respect of persons. The sinner has been followed into all his hiding places. Every mask has been torn off from the moralist and self-righteous. The deceitfulness of the heart has been exposed; and the sinner has been met at every turn, with the naked sword of the Spirit pointed at his breast.

6. Union of feeling and effort in churches had promoted this revival. Where the great body of the church has come up to the help of the Lord, the work has been powerful: And although there have been in most of the churches, some who have stood all the day idle; yet a larger proportion have manifested a deep interest in the work than in former revivals. The coldness or the opposition of professors, has been found far more injurious than the opposition of others.

7. Meetings of inquiry have been greatly blessed. As the nature of these meetings is generally understood, and as the manner in which they have been conducted in this revival, has been in a measure described in the preceding accounts, it is unnecessary to say more.

8. Avoiding disputes upon minor points. Care has been taken to guard Christians against all sectarian feelings. In some instances injury has been done; but we believe that the churches generally have done less to grieve the Spirit, by any improper conduct, in this respect, than is common in revivals. Indeed we may say, that, with few exceptions, churches of different names have felt and manifested more solicitude to make converts than proselytes.

9. Urging awakened sinners to *immediate* repentance and reconciliation to God. No excuse, on account of human depravity, or human dependence and divine agency, has been allowed. To all such objections, a "thus saith the Lord," has been the reply. Where instruction was needed, the nature and reasonableness of these duties have been fully pointed out. If the impenitent have still pleaded any excuse, they have been told that the controversy was between them and God, and with him they must settle it. The effect of this mode of address, generally, has been, that conviction has increased, until the sinner has surrendered himself into the hands of a Holy, sovereign and merciful God.

10. The visits of ministers, professors and others, where revivals had commenced, have had a powerful effect in extending the work. Ministers and private Christians have thus been refreshed. When they returned home, they have told others, and exhorted their brethren to awake. Sinners have in many

cases returned, rejoicing in hope, or deeply convicted. Thus the holy fire has spread and blazed in every direction.

11. The preaching and other labours of evangelists have been a very obvious and efficient means of originating and carrying forward the work. Ministers have thus received essential assistance.

12. United, agonizing, persevering prayer. This has evidently been one of the principal means, which God has blessed, in originating and extending this work of grace.

13. The instructions given in Sabbath schools and Bible classes have been eminently blessed. A large number of those who belong to our Sabbath schools give satisfactory evidence of piety. Superintendents and teachers have in many cases been the honoured instruments of their conversion. In several instances, most of the members of Bible classes have become converts, and promise to be among the most stable and valuable members of our churches; and should Bible classes and Sabbath schools continue to multiply, as they have done a few years past, we may hope the time will soon arrive when most of the rising generation will be converted in youth, and that the violent "stirs" now raised against revivals, will cease for want of materials.

SELECT BIBLIOGRAPHY

Cross, Whitney Rogers. *The Burned-Over District: The Social and Intellectual History of Enthusiastic Religion in Western New York, 1800-1850*. Ithaca, N.Y.: Cornell University Press, 1950. Rpt., New York: Harper & Row, 1965.

Finney, Charles G. *Memoirs*. New York: A. S. Barnes, 1872.

McLoughlin, William G. *Modern Revivalism: Charles Grandison Finney to Billy Graham*. New York: Ronald Press, 1959.

Tyler, Bennet. *Memoir of the Life and Character of Rev. Asahel Nettleton, D.D.* Hartford: Robins & Smith, 1844.

Weisberger, Bernard A. *They Gathered at the River: The Story of the Great Revivalists and Their Impact upon Religion in America*. Boston: Little, Brown, 1958.

Part Three
Religious Adolescence

During the latter half of the nineteenth century and the early decades of the twentieth, American religion in many respects resembled a developing teenager. Spurts of growth continued in some Christian communions, producing an overall sense of undiminished progress. The uneven pattern of growth, however, produced also a gangling appearance—perhaps fairly representing the reality. More important, deep ambiguities in matters of theology and practice enveloped portions of American Christianity. Unbounded optimism met recalcitrant belief systems; new directions met innate spiritual conservatism. One could even argue that the overall configuration suffered a corporate identity crisis of sorts. Not only did Christians in the United States find themselves on both sides of the Civil conflagration of the 1860s, but they also discovered that their faith yielded different attitudes toward the world itself, especially as the sciences grew to view it. Moral reforms from earlier decades yielded new implications as time went by. The antislavery work of women led them to consider their own plight, for example. Susan B. Anthony, Amelia Bloomer, and many others of the suffragist leaders began as agitators for abolition or temperance. Such work led Sarah and Angelina Grimke, Elizabeth Cady Stanton, and others to oppose traditional religious affiliations in America.

Abraham Lincoln may have captured a portion of the sense of fragmentation in his declaration (or lament) that "both sides read the same Bible and pray to the same God." The poignancy of the situation did not abate with nightfall, as hostile camps could hear each other singing gospel hymns in the wartime revivals among Union and Confederate armies that flourished in the face of battles. Torn churches, divided families, only scattered evidences of grace—America's thriving sense of unmitigated promise crumbled.

Black Americans could surely take heart in their liberation from slavery. Captains of industry and immigrants benefited to some degree from the wartime economy. And Horace Bushnell, good theologian that he was, perceived in the war a time of sacrifice that held the potential of making the whole people more open to God. In general, however, the war years only served to shatter the dreams of mainstream American religion and lead most of its leaders to adopt a rather narrow identification with parochial interests.

Reconstruction offered a promising situation to some previously unfranchised citizens, but it proved to be a period of scant improvement for most Americans. Congregationalists, Presbyterians, Methodists, and Baptists in the North turned at least temporarily to radical Republicanism. Those in the South dined on bitterness. White Southern Protestants became increasingly regional in their worldview, and the "Bible Belt" began to offer baptism of the "Lost Cause" and the "Southern Way of Life." Southern Baptists, Southern Methodists, and Southern Presbyterians in particular justified their existence during Reconstruction in terms of God's calling people out of the world into a "spiritual church." The appeal of the South encompassed former border states that "waited until after Appomatox to join the Confederacy." A destructive sense of parochial identity continued schisms among Christians long after the nation had become a "Reunited States."

American life became more complex in a bewildering variety of different yet interrelated aspects. Frontier chaos gradually diminished, with a corresponding loss in vitality. A rapid industrialization affected patterns in family life, people's sense of vocation, demographics, and the nation's class structure. The invention of the radio revolutionized communication. "New" sources of energy and new ways to manipulate the environment were discovered and exploited. Trade and mission overtures reached into a variety of different areas. And the list goes on.

During 1869, to take just one example, America finally adjudicated claims with England resulting from the Civil War and settling a long-standing question about national viability for the former colony. At the same time, a fifteenth amendment to the U.S. Constitution passed which promised black citizens the right to vote. The country survived the fracas between railroad czars, the "Erie War," which had threatened the base of capitalism. Meanwhile President Grant agitated for Cuban independence from Spain, sought avenues of entrance to the Mikado's Japan, and worried about the opening of the Suez Canal—new, cosmopolitan concerns reflecting national aspirations to world power. In the same year the Union Pacific opened transcontinental service, and speculation on gold brought fortune to a few but ruin to many.

Also during 1869, American Catholics greeted the promise of a Vatican Council with mixed feelings. Pope Pius IX convoked the ecumenical gathering to address the question of papal infallibility. Many of the faithful desired simple answers for this complex problem. Most of the American hierarchy, however, felt that pronouncements on the subject would do more harm than good, that a doctrinal formulation of this sort would cut off the dialogue on pluralistic allegiance they hoped for in the U.S.

Harvard, still the epitome of the American educational enterprise in 1869, elected as president Charles William Eliot, an avowed proponent of evolutionary theory. Charles Darwin had published the *Origin of Species* a decade earlier, in 1859. One major American scientist, Louis Agassiz, had popularized contrary "explanations" of the presence of fossils and of the resemblances among various categories of living things. The triumph of Eliot and the defeat of Agassiz and others in the contest for leadership of Harvard's intellectual milieu signaled a new era of scientific ascendancy in American thought.

Consider the impact of all these and the myriad other events upon the lives of Christians and communions. Nor was 1869 a special or unrepresentative year in the life of adolescent America; it was just another, like all the rest that together compounded possibilities and problems for people. Some embraced one or more of the possibilities in search of new meaning. Others responded to one or more of the problems, either by retreating or by trying various solutions.

Millennialists, though not so popular in the latter decades of the nineteenth century as previously under William Miller, preached the coming rapture to release "real" Christians from the world (with its complexity). Other conservative evangelicals struggled to consolidate a doctrine of biblical authority that would emphasize the unique place of Scripture in the lives of Christians. The prophecy and Bible conferences of the late 1800s, held periodically in resort areas of the country, sought to combine millennial interests with an espousal of verbal inerrancy of the Bible. The evangelistic ministry of Dwight L. Moody likewise pointed thousands of Christians toward the Bible as its own best interpreter. In "Bible Readings," sermons that related a text in circular fashion to many diverse passages of Scripture, people could speak and hear a gospel message uninterrupted by the complicated demands of the modern world. Moreover, the inner authority of Scripture could be simply stated and simply held. It sounded deeply traditional, a "rock on a storm-tossed sea."

The simplicity of essential Christianity became even more of a reality for many with the rise of a movement termed "Fundamentalism." Only a few doctrines stood at the core of the faith in this worldview—inerrancy of Scripture and Christ's virgin birth, atonement, resurrection, and power to work miracles, according to one list that Presbyterians adopted. Others held that it was essential for all believers to affirm the second coming as well. Various groups drew up various lists of "Fundamentals," but they all offered a means by which millions of Christians sought to make their faith manageable, reducing its ambiguities by reducing the complexity of its theology.

Large numbers of Christians proceeded in a contrary manner, accepting the modern situation as God's gift and embracing scientific insights as applicable to the faith. Asa Gray, for example, accentuated the harmony of evolutionary theory with Christian doctrine. William Graham Sumner formed his work *Folkways* around a sense of the inevitability of classes and other forms of human inequality learned over evolutionary eons. Left-wing Unitarians formed a Free Religious Association in 1865 to foster the ideas of a "scientific theism" first enunciated by Theodore Parker. Mary Baker Eddy also sought to institute scientific methods in religious life with her movement, as did Charles and Myrtle Fillmore with their concentration on spiritual harmony institutionalized in Unity Temples that rose in many cities across the country. And the New Thought Alliance and the movement that came to be known as "Jehovah's Witnesses" were just two of the many other groups that began during this time, either centered in the United States or spilling over from European beginnings.

Still another segment of American Christians sought neither reduction of the faith nor immense changes in it. They tried rather to "hold fast to what is good," as Charles Hodge quoted Scripture. He, his son A. A. Hodge, and other Calvinists typified that mentality. Hodge declared at Princeton Theological Seminary that he wanted to "change nothing" in the tradition that offered Christians so full a life in the church. Segments of other traditions—Lutheran, Episcopalian, Catholic—worked to retain their own distinctiveness against the same pressures for change that came especially from those who felt the mainstream had come to embody a religious elitism in America. The "Social Gospel" arose to challenge traditional Christian practice as well as the older doctrines.

Proponents of the Social Gospel sought to remake human existence in accord with what they considered the essence of Jesus' teachings. They held that people, social relationships, and institutions should all reflect the process of redemption in daily activity. Salvation had been promised by God and had to be claimed in order to transform the world in love.

Horace Bushnell influenced the beginnings of America's social cri-tique of society by emphasizing the need for long-term nurture for Christians. Nurture produced mature Christian disciples, not revival "flash-in-the-pan believers." The call by some British Christians for new patterns of Christian socialism that would accentuate cooperation more than competition also made an impact upon American religious leaders. Other liberal strains of thought—transcendentalism, for example—continued to hold some sway in helping pave the way for a Social Gospel.

Washington Gladden, a pastor throughout his ministry, first in Massachusetts and then in Columbus, Ohio, called for the application of Christian principles to the situation of workers and the indigent in society. He was determined that the church could and would supply the moral undergirding to enable such a humane change in the social structures.

Cardinal Gibbons of Baltimore also made eloquent appeals in behalf of the poor and the recent immigrants in America. He and other liberal Catholics stood with forces of democracy as they applied to matters of both church and state. Gibbons defended the Knights of Labor and other societies of workers that telescoped the coming of powerful trade unions in the United States.

The primary formulator of the Social Gospel, however, was the Baptist minister and theologian Walter Rauschenbusch. A dedicated Christian, Rauschenbusch served many years as pastor to the ethnic population in which he had grown up—the German working folk in the Hell's Kitchen section of New York City. He gradually developed a critique of capitalism from a biblical perspective that argued for a dawning "Kingdom of Righteousness" that would encompass the entire social and political life of the people. This was what the prophets and what Jesus himself had proclaimed, said Rauschenbusch: a place of humanity and justice. In the face of Fundamentalist claims that they had defined the essence of Christianity, he offered in 1917 another list of five "funda mentals"—social justice, collective property rights, industrial democracy, approximate equality, and cooperation.

Subsequent events have thrown into some disrepute the exuberance of Rauschenbusch and his colleagues in propounding a social gospel, but historians evaluate the movement as perhaps the most distinctive American theological enterprise yet offered. But the era was as much characterized by movement in the direction of the Fundamentalists as by the movement of the Social Gospel in precisely the opposite direction. The vigor of both Modernism and Traditionalism at the same time makes it difficult to describe a simple overall pattern. Historians have found it impossible to construct a clear identity for religious institutions in the period except among a few "true believers" and their small constituencies.

Another sense of direction for American Christianity can be gleaned from looking at the philosophical pragmatism of the era. Although it does injustice to the finer points in the thought of William James, John Dewey, and others in the "American school of philosophy," it can be said generally that pragmatism became a guiding principle throughout much of the country.

Missionaries exhibited a particular interest in the question "Does it work?" Methodist William Wesley Van Orsdel was one such missionary, ministering among the simple miners and farmers in the Midwest and in the mountains. He epitomized the new breed of circuit rider in American Methodism, the gentle, God-fearing, hard-working missionary who graduated in later years from riding his chestnut horse to driving his Model-T Ford. Sheldon Jackson provided the same kind of pragmatic emphasis for the Presbyterians, forming new churches in the West and in Alaskan outposts. Unafraid of a possible conflict of interest between church and state, he served as both *sine titulo* "bishop" for the Presbyterians and U.S. administrator of education at the same time. Other denominations had similar rough-and-ready folk willing to do whatever would bring Christianity to the people of the expanding frontier.

Revivalists also asked "Does it work?" as they sought the conversion of both church folk and the unchurched in America's more populated areas. Dwight L. Moody personified this quest. He built on the methods and techniques of Charles G. Finney, who had introduced such innovations as "protracted meetings" and the "anxious bench" in his revivals. Moody likewise apprenticed himself to British evangelists before leading crusades himself both in England and in the United States. Moody's revival campaigns brought in thousands of souls to the churches. If it worked, Moody used it—prayer meetings, "Bible Readings," massed choirs, snappy phrases, anti-intellectualism, dramatic pulpit actions, inquiry rooms for the "almost persuaded," and so on. He sought to revive the churches and to bring America to Christ by saving the unchurched at the same time.

Pentecostalism also burst upon the American scene, though many of its outward manifestations resembled the spiritual "exercises" of previous eras. From Los Angeles to New York, from Chicago to south Florida, millennial expectations, charismatic expressions, and healing services characterized increasingly vast portions of religious consciousness.

Businessmen—they were almost all men—came to lead the church both from religious conviction and from a sense that it would help commercial prospects. Moody himself came from a business background into evangelism. Businessman John Wannamaker supported him. John D. Rockefeller, James Duke, and other captains of industry underwrote much of the activity of church movements and personages—albeit in very distinctive ways and toward somewhat different ends.

And the United States grew. How it grew! It moved into the intrigue and horror of World War I as a belated but full partner in the fray. The Great War served both to sober the nation and to push America toward maturity.

73810

Susan B. Anthony and the Rights of Women

This case was prepared by Samuel Garrett

In 1853 the New York State Teachers' Association held its annual convention at Rochester, New York. Presiding was Charles Davies, LL.D., professor of mathematics at West Point and well-known author of textbooks. The meeting moved to consider "Why the profession of teacher is not respected as that of doctor, lawyer, or minister." Although a large number of the teachers present were women, they did not speak at such meetings. Suddenly, however, Miss Susan B. Anthony of Rochester, an experienced teacher in various girls' schools who had recently retired as girls' headmistress at the Canajoharie Academy, rose in her place.

"Mr. President," she said to the chair.

"What will the lady have?" he asked, in the midst of a shocked silence.

"I wish to speak to the question under discussion," Miss Anthony replied.

The president of the convention was willing to entertain a motion to that effect, which one of the men in the meeting thereupon made. Then, for a half hour or so, it was debated whether Miss Anthony should be allowed to speak. She remained standing silently in her place through it all, lest she lose her chance to speak. It was noted that she was not wearing the tight-waisted hoop skirt then in fashion but one of the new costumes named for Mrs. Amelia Bloomer: a short loose-fitting skirt worn over a pair of baggy trousers down to the ankles. When the debate had worn itself out, the motion was passed in her favor by a small margin, and then Miss Anthony had her say.

It seems to me you fail to comprehend the cause of the disrespect of which you complain. Do you not see that so long as society says woman has not brains enough to be a doctor, lawyer, or minister, but has plenty to be a teacher, every man of you who condescends to teach tacitly admits before all Israel and the sun that he has no more brains than a woman?

She sat down.

At the meeting the next day, Professor Davies spoke in his flowery manner, suggesting that pure chivalry and the wish to protect female teachers was the reason that they had never been invited to speak or take part in committee work in the Association. A Mrs. Northrop of Rochester then stood up, got the floor with some difficulty, and introduced a resolution to the effect that the Teachers' Association recognize "the rights of female teachers to share in all the privileges and deliberations of this body." She also referred to the inadequate salaries paid to the women teachers: $2.50 a week, compared to the $10.00 a week for the men. The president tried to ignore the resolution, but the combined votes of the female delegates and the "more liberal" men were enough to pass it. Once more Miss Anthony, a quiet, rather diffident Quaker, had gotten something started. What did it mean?

AMERICAN FRIENDS

Susan Brownell Anthony was born 14 February 1820 to a family in Adams, a town in the far northwestern corner of Massachusetts. Her father's people had been farmers—and Quakers—for generations, seeking out the more isolated areas in which to live the Quaker way of life removed as far as possible from the ways of the "world." Still, Susan's father, Daniel Anthony, had received a good education at the Quaker school at Nine Partners, in Dutchess County, New York. His sister Hannah had gained some renown in the community as a Quaker preacher. Their mother also served as an elder in the Meeting they attended.

Daniel Anthony was not entirely a conventional Quaker type, particularly not as a younger man. The Meeting had seriously conferred with him when he had made known his resolve to marry outside the fold, a musical, vivacious woman named Lucy Read, who belonged to a Baptist family in the neighboring town of Cheshire. Lucy was willing to take on the Quaker ways, although she never joined the Meeting. The story goes that she danced all night for the last time at a party two or three days before her marriage, after which she would dance no more; even her music would henceforth be frowned on. Her new husband, however, was enterprising and resourceful, and instead of staying with farming, he built himself a small cloth mill by a stream, the first in the region, and hired the neighboring farm girls to tend the looms. Then, when Susan was still a small child, he took his family over into New York State, to Battenville, where he went into partnership to operate a larger mill and a larger cloth business.

Daniel Anthony held a number of strong convictions. Soon after his marriage he got into trouble with the Meeting for selling liquor, as a result of which he "reformed" overnight and became an active worker in the temperance movement. In common with most Quakers, he refused to vote at elections, since he could not recognize a government that waged war. He refused to pay taxes for the same reason; when the tax collector came around, he would take out his wallet, lay it on his desk, and tell the man to take out of it—to "rob" him of—whatever he wanted. Later Daniel developed a serious concern about the whole institution of slavery. In the early 1830s, when Elias Hicks led a portion of the Quaker fellowship that emphatically opposed slavery and favored the new abolitionist program, Daniel Anthony heartily joined his fellowship. This was, as a whole, a more liberal movement among Quakers, reemphasizing the teaching of the Inner Light and playing down the more orthodox stress on the authority of Scripture. Most of the Quaker meetings in the upper New York State area went over to the Hicksite side, and meetings used to be held on Sunday in the Anthony's fine Battenville house.

Susan was the second daughter of a family of five girls and two boys. She was influenced by her father's interests and convictions but also by her mother's now rather quiet and reserved sense of not fully belonging to her husband's way. She also received a good education outside of the home—something both parents agreed was important for all of their children. Susan followed her older sister in 1837 to Miss Moulson's Seminary in Philadelphia, a Quaker school in which the country girl's interests in mathematics and science had a chance to develop. In 1839, however, Daniel's business in Battenville finally failed in the midst of an economic depression, and Susan had to go to work as a teacher, at the standard $2.50 a week salary. For a time she taught school at New Rochelle, New York. Later she moved closer to Center Falls, where the family had moved. Daniel tried to support his family with various odd jobs, such as logging and teaching schools, and all the children contributed in various ways to the meager income. Once more Daniel got into trouble with the Meeting, this time for keeping a dance hall for the young people of the neighborhood. The Meeting was not impressed by the fact that he diligently forbade the drinking of any liquor on the premises. When Daniel refused to obey the Meeting, he was "disowned," and ceased to be a member from then on.

At length the Reads, Lucy Anthony's Baptist relatives, came to the rescue. Joshua Read, one of Lucy's brothers, provided the Anthonys with a place to live on a farm he owned outside the town of Rochester; the family moved there in November 1845, traveling "out West" by way of the Erie Canal. The following spring Susan was appointed headmistress for girls (under the authority, of course, of the boys' headmaster, or principal) at the Canajoharie Academy, of which Joshua Read was a trustee. Here she had a good salary, congenial friends, and some status of her own for the first time in her life. She was an attractive, even impressive, person, who enjoyed fine clothes and the association with her "worldly" Read cousins.

Above all she enjoyed her independence, particularly the chance to engage in some worthwhile social project—temperance. She became active in the Canajoharie chapter of the New York Daughters of Temperance, eventually serving as president of the chapter. She also enjoyed the parties and dances in which her cousins and their friends shared, although she seemed to disapprove heartily of the fact that so many of the young men drank whiskey. She turned down a number of marriage proposals. One of her suitors, a good friend of earlier years, Aaron McLean, son of her father's business partner in Battenville, married her older sister instead.

The Anthony family out in Rochester, in the meantime, had also entered upon better times, developing interests that characteristically represented a good deal of social usefulness. Daniel Anthony did not try for long to keep up the farm, for it was too small to support his family. Instead he was taken on as one of the first agents in the area for the New York Life Insurance Company, and he prospered greatly in the new position, losing only his independence. A number of Quaker families lived in the Rochester area, almost all of them Hicksite, keenly interested in the temperance movement, and zealous for the abolition of slavery. Daniel Anthony seemed to have "come home" at last, and he entered into the challenge of a whole new intellectual world.

Some of the persons active in this community are worth noting. The abolitionist leader and former slave Frederick Douglass settled in Rochester and edited his newspaper, *The North Star,* there. There were also a number of subscribers in Rochester to William Lloyd Garrison's *Liberator* and to the *Anti-Slavery Standard.* In nearby Syracuse lived the Reverend Samuel J. May, a Unitarian minister and advocate of various social reforms, with whom Daniel Anthony became a close friend. William Henry Channing, nephew of the famous Unitarian minister William Ellery Channing and himself a minister of that denomination as

well as an active abolitionist, provided a congenial church for the Anthonys to attend for a time. And Daniel himself was continually offering
hospitality to other like-minded and often even more famous people who
passed through Rochester: Garrison himself, Wendell Phillips, and others. This was also the time that many were addressing the question of
whether to help fugitive slaves seeking to cross the border into Canada.
The Anthony farm, close to a town that was in turn close to the Canadian
border, was an ideal "station" on the New York underground railway.

In the midst of all this, Daniel Anthony and his family learned of the
woman's rights convention scheduled for 19-20 July 1848 in the town of
Seneca Falls, halfway between Rochester and Syracuse. A prominent
abolitionist leader, Henry Stanton, and his wife, Elizabeth Cady Stanton,
were sponsors of the convention. Two weeks after the meetings at Seneca
Falls, a session took place at Rochester at which area Quakers turned out
in full force to sign the "Declaration of Woman's Rights" (including the
clear demand for the vote for women urged by Elizabeth Cady Stanton)
that had been drawn up at the Seneca Falls meeting. The national woman's rights movement was born, with Daniel and Lucy Anthony and their
youngest daughter, Mary, among the charter members.

In Canajoharie that summer, Susan Anthony was chiefly interested
in the circus. She found woman's rights "amusing" and was more
inclined to write to her family about having attended "The Greatest
Show on Earth," to which she wore her "blue lawn dress, and the gypsy
hat with roses under the brim"! Shortly after this she visited her parents at
Rochester for the first time since her job had begun, but she stayed only
for a week. She did not move back to Rochester until the fall of 1849. A
new, uncongenial principal (the son of an Alabama slaveholder) had been
put over her at the Academy. Her father communicated the stress and
excitement of abolitionist activities to her in his letters. She had begun to
feel a restlessness with life, wishing even that she could go off to California to search for gold.

COMMITMENT

On her return to Rochester, Susan continued to feel restless and direc-
tionless. She had saved three hundred dollars during fifteen years of
teaching. She agreed to run the farm while her father looked after his
insurance business over at Syracuse and she did some substitute teaching
in the Rochester schools. Apparently her father encouraged her to think
of taking up the work of a social reformer, for even if she did marry (and

he hoped she would), "Quaker women were not handicapped by marital status." So Susan Anthony began to branch out, not only helping to run her parents' house and joining the Rochester chapter of the Daughters of Temperance but also listening to the guests who stayed with her family as they discussed the issues of the day. She gradually made up her mind to take her stand with her father and his friends.

One day in May 1851, returning from a temperance convention to the east, she was passing through Seneca Falls and stayed for a few nights at the home of Mrs. Amelia Bloomer, editor and publisher of a newspaper called *The Lily*, "devoted to the Interests of Women." Mrs. Bloomer's main interest at the time was temperance—hence the friendship with Susan. But Susan knew that William Lloyd Garrison and an English abolitionist, George Thompson, were scheduled to lecture in Seneca Falls at that time, and she wanted to hear them. Elizabeth Cady Stanton was also a resident of Seneca Falls. She and her husband were to be hosts to the visitors. Mrs. Bloomer and Mrs. Stanton were not on very close terms, the latter's involvement in the woman's rights movement having proved troublesome to the former. It turned out, however, that as the Stantons were returning from the lectures with Garrison and Thompson they met Mrs. Bloomer and Miss Anthony in the street and struck up a friendship.

A few weeks later Mrs. Stanton invited Susan and Lucy Stone, another ardent woman's rights advocate, to her home to confer with Horace Greeley of the New York City *Tribune* on a plan for coeducation. Nothing came of the plan, but of the meeting there came a great deal. Mrs. Stanton (always so called by her new friend and associate) and Susan B. Anthony became firm friends and co-workers in the woman's rights movement for the rest of their lives, a period of over fifty years.

Miss Anthony continued her temperance movement activities. In January 1852, the Sons of Temperance held a mass meeting in Albany, and she attended with other representatives of the Rochester chapter of the Daughters of Temperance. During the meeting she rose to speak to a motion and was told by the "chairman" that "the Sisters were not invited there to speak, but to listen and learn." Susan promptly walked out of the hall, followed by a few of the other women. She then turned to organizing a Woman's State Temperance Society for New York, of which she managed to get Mrs. Stanton elected president. That summer, however, at the Syracuse convention of the Men's Society, in spite of support from the Reverend Samuel J. May, a Unitarian minister friend of Daniel Anthony, the women's temperance organization was not allowed to speak. The temperance movement, it appeared, was controlled by the clergy and other churchmen who held that "it was not decent for a woman to speak in public on any subject whatsoever, even on a moral issue." Only Greeley's *Tribune* supported the women publicly.

When the Women's State Temperance Society convention in June 1853 failed to reelect Mrs. Stanton as president, fearing the reaction of public opinion to her stand on woman's suffrage and her advocacy of making drunkenness grounds for divorce, Susan resigned as secretary from the organization as well. Indeed, the whole women's temperance movement died down in New York State. Women's rights, and particularly the vote for women, became a burning cause for Susan B. Anthony. She took her first active part in that cause at the Third National Woman's Rights Convention, held at Syracuse in September 1852. A gathering of present and future leaders in the movement, such as Lucretia Mott (with her husband, James Mott), Lucy Stone, the Reverend Antoinette Brown, and a host of others, the Convention provided Susan B. Anthony with hope.

WOMAN'S RIGHTS

Why the second third of the nineteenth century in the United States should have produced such a rapid growth of the woman's rights movement is something of a mystery. It is commonly suggested that it was one aspect of a larger body of social changes produced by the industrial revolution, involving as it did such things as the hiring of substantial numbers of farm girls to work in the cloth mills. Other scholars attribute it to Enlightenment liberalism, although it is not clear why the issue of woman's rights should have lagged behind other liberal concerns by the space of a generation or more. More recent analyses contend that it came in reaction to the tyranny of the conjugal or nuclear family, which became a new force in the nineteenth century as the loosely organized though indispensable extended family was replaced by a strictly defined nucleus, creating a mystique of woman and her rightful place. Still other scholars argue that the woman's movement grew in reaction to a social situation that extended back considerably farther than just the early years of the nineteenth century. Some contend that women were assigned an inferior position in society at the time of the Reformation, when family life was emphasized in contrast to monasticism (women had ruled in certain medieval monastic communities, including some in which both men and women were members). Others date the beginning of the oppression of women to the beginning of the so-called "dark ages," or even to the time of the ancient world of the Mediterranean community.

Whatever the origins of the oppression, in nineteenth-century Europe and America, women became more conscious that they were being treated as inferiors in all but a few areas open to them. They also became more convinced of the need to resist that oppression.

In considering the background and influences operating on the woman's rights movement, students of the subject note the following:

• A close connection of the movement with that of the abolitionists. Frequently leaders of one took part in the other as well. The abolitionists' tactics in particular were known, for example, in the pages of Garrison's *Liberator*:

> I will be as harsh as truth, and as uncompromising as justice. On this subject I do not wish to think, or speak, or write, with moderation. . . . I am in earnest—I will not equivocate—I will not excuse—I will not retreat a single inch—AND I WILL BE HEARD.

• A theological background of the woman's rights movement (as well as that of abolitionism) in seventeenth-century radical Puritanism, particularly in Quakerism but also in the revival movement that began in the late 1820s in New York State's "burned-over" region. Charles G. Finney, a leader of the revival movement, founded coeducational Oberlin College as an important center. The Reverend Antoinette Brown proved an important representative of the movement.
• A sharp opposition to conventional Christianity. The opposition was especially apparent in the work of Sarah Moore Grimke and her sister Angelina, Lucy Stone, and above all Elizabeth Cady Stanton, with her "Woman's Bible."
• An awareness of laws on the books that discriminated against women, particularly those dealing with marriage and divorce, and the difficulty of changing such laws and providing for new ones without wider support in the body politic based on a truly universal suffrage.

PARTNERSHIP

All of this seemed to be reflected in the experience of Susan B. Anthony. The movement's historical background is largely her own; the debate over the suffrage issue was an important feature of her life following her "conversion" to the cause in the early 1850s. The personal interest of her story, as well as the work which the movement accomplished, comes through most clearly in the context of the working relationship Miss Anthony had with the older, more radical, more experienced, and even more creative Elizabeth Cady Stanton.

Consider, for example, Miss Anthony's letter to Mrs. Stanton in which she indicates her intentions concerning the upcoming New York State Teachers' Association convention:

> During July I want to speak certainly twice at Avon, Clifton and Sharon and Ballston Springs and Lake George—Now will you load my gun, leaving me only to pull the trigger and let fly the powder and ball—Don't delay one mail to tell me what you will do—for I must not and will not allow those school masters to say—See, these women can't or won't do anything when we do give them a chance—No they shan't say that, even if I have to get a man to write it—but no man can write from my stand point, nor no woman but you—for all, all would base their strongest argument on the unlikeness of the sexes. . . .

SELECTED BIBLIOGRAPHY

Anthony, Katharine. *Susan B. Anthony: Her Personal History and Her Era.* Garden City, N.Y.: Doubleday, 1954.

Dorr, Rheta Childe. *Susan B. Anthony: The Woman Who Changed the Mind of a Nation.* New York: Frederick A. Stokes, 1928.

Flexner, Eleanor. *Century of Struggle: The Woman's Rights Movement in the United States.* New York: Atheneum, 1972.

Harper, Ida Husted. *The Life and Work of Susan B. Anthony: A Story of the Evolution in the Status of Woman.* 3 vols. Indianapolis: Bowen-Merrill, 1898; Indianapolis: The Hollenbeck Press, 1908.

Martin, Wendy, ed. *The American Sisterhood: Writings of the Feminist Movement from Colonial Times to the Present.* New York: Harper & Row, 1972.

Stanton, Elizabeth Cady; Susan B. Anthony; and Matilda Joslyn Gage, eds. *History of Woman Suffrage.* 3 Vols.: 1848-85. Rochester, N.Y.: Susan B. Anthony, 1889.

Abraham Lincoln and American Civil Religion

This case was prepared by Douglas H. Gregg

The sky was gray and a light rain fell as the 1865 Inaugural parade churned its way up muddy Pennsylvania Avenue from the White House to the Capitol. Four white horses led the way, hauling a model of a Navy Monitor on wheels, its small cannon blazing with salutes. Civic and patriotic groups followed, banners waving. For the first time in Washington a battalion of black troops in Union Army dress marched as inaugural guards, and in line with them came the Negro Grand Lodge of Odd Fellows. There was a holiday mood among the growing crowds of people. By ten in the morning, the throng at the eastern front of the Capitol, where the Inaugural was to take place at two o'clock, reached well beyond the approaches to the Capitol's eastern portico.

Joseph Graves stamped his feet and rubbed his hands to keep warm. He had arrived early, determined to secure an advantageous place from which to see and hear the President take his second oath of office. He was equally determined that he should greet the President personally that evening at the White House reception. Perhaps there he could quickly ask him one or two questions. Feeling his notepad and pen in one pocket, Joseph remembered his official reason for enduring the cold wait—his promise to write a personal news account of the Inaugural, and especially of Lincoln's religious views, for his town newspaper in Indiana. He smiled, remembering the editor's final words to him: "Clarify as best you can the President's religious notions, for surely he's as slippery as an eel and obtuse to the point of distraction when it comes to lining himself up with some acceptable Christian group."

It hadn't taken much encouragement to get Joseph to make the two-day train trip to Washington. He had followed Lincoln's public career closely since the time of the debates with Stephen Douglas and found that his growing interest in Lincoln had slowly turned to deep admiration. He liked the President's penchant for storytelling and humor. Abe Lincoln could laugh at himself, which was a refreshing contrast to the stuffiness and pumped-up self-important airs most politicians exhibited. Joseph nearly laughed out loud remembering the story of two Quaker women overheard in conversation on a railway coach:

"I think Jefferson Davis will succeed."
"Why does thee think so?"
"Because Jefferson is a praying man."
"And so is Abraham a praying man."
"Yes, but the Lord will think Abraham is joking."

What most drew Joseph to Lincoln, however, was that he found in Lincoln something of the same suspicion and mild antagonism toward organized religion that Joseph felt so strongly himself. He agreed with Lincoln that local churches "neglected the fundamental love of God and of neighbor by too much introverted attention upon correctness in theological opinion." But Joseph was puzzled by Lincoln's affinity for Scripture. Lincoln continually interpreted the nation's history—especially the war—in the light of biblical motifs of judgment, punishment, justice, mercy, and reconciliation. Yet it was the Declaration of Independence that had, by Lincoln's own admission, the force of revelation for him. Then too, there was Lincoln's apparently strong attraction toward the Christian Savior. Was Lincoln a Christian, as some claimed, or an infidel of the worst sort as many others had charged? Were his frequent public references to the Divine Sovereignty and to American destiny under God simply for show, to please the crowds, or were they rooted in some deep authentically religious understanding of himself and the nation as instruments of God's will? And if the latter, was it wisdom or arrogance that saw the United States as God's almost chosen people called to a special vocation of preserving and extending freedom and self-government?

Perhaps he would have some answers to his questions by evening. In the meantime, it was warming a bit, and the time of waiting was nearly half over. Joseph glanced at those around him, all preoccupied in conversation and banter. Taking out the small lunch he had brought with him, he began to review the events in Lincoln's life that would provide helpful background for the article he was to write.

EARLY LIFE AND CAREER

Abraham Lincoln was born 12 February 1809 in a backwoods cabin three miles south of Hodgenville, Kentucky. When he was six years old, his family moved to southwestern Indiana, where his father, Thomas, established a farm on public land. Lincoln received little formal education. He once said that he had gone to school "by littles"—a little now and a little then—so that his entire schooling amounted to about a year's attendance. Still, he managed to learn to read and write. Books were hard to come by, but as a youth he read Parson Weem's *Life of Washington* (with its story of the little hatchet and the cherry tree), *Robinson Crusoe, Pilgrim's Progress,* and Aesop's Fables, along with the Bible.

In 1830, the Lincoln family migrated again, this time to Illinois. Lincoln was twenty-one, six-feet-four-inches tall, rawboned and lanky, muscular and physically powerful, good-natured and talented as a mimic and storyteller. Noted for the skill and strength with which he could use an ax, he spoke with a backwoods twang and walked in the long-striding, flatfooted manner of a plowman.

In Illinois, Lincoln tried a variety of occupations. As a "rail splitter," he helped to clear and fence his father's new farm. As a flatboatman, he made a voyage down the Mississippi River to New Orleans. He eventually settled in New Salem, a village of about twenty-five families on the Sangamon River. He worked there as a storekeeper, postmaster, and surveyor. He enlisted as a volunteer in the Black Hawk War of 1832 and later joked that he had seen no fighting Indians during the war but had had "a good many bloody struggles with the mosquitoes." He finally decided to study law. He passed the bar exams in 1836 and moved the following year to Springfield, where he established a successful law practice. Following a lengthy courtship, he married Mary Todd in 1842.

Lincoln was repeatedly elected to the Illinois state legislature between 1834 and 1842, and he served a single term in Congress from 1847 to 1849. His political career seemed at an end in the early 1850s, but the deepening sectional crisis gave him opportunity to reemerge in political life and rise to leadership. In a series of debates with Stephen A. Douglas, his rival for a Senate seat in 1858, Lincoln pushed home his views that slavery should be contained and should not be extended to the territories—that "a house divided against itself cannot stand," that the "government cannot endure permanently half slave and half free," that the country would eventually become "all one thing, or all the other." Lincoln believed that the civil liberties of every U.S. citizen, white as well as black, were at stake and that the territories must be kept free, because the new free states were "places for poor people to go and better their condition."

Though he failed to win the Senate seat, Lincoln gained national recognition and began to be mentioned as a presidential prospect for 1860. At the Republican national convention Lincoln was nominated on the third ballot to be the Republican candidate for president. In the national election, with the Republicans united and the Democrats divided and a total of four candidates in the field, he carried the election.

RELIGIOUS BELIEF AND AFFILIATION

Lincoln attended Presbyterian services in Springfield and later in Washington, but he never joined any church. He once explained: "When any church will inscribe over its altar the Savior's condensed statement of law and gospel: 'Thou shalt love the Lord thy God with all thy heart, and with all thy soul and with all thy mind, and love thy neighbor as thyself,' that church I will join with all my heart." In his early political career he had often been accused of being a skeptic and freethinker, and he once complained that the "church influence" was used against him. When running for Congress in 1846, he issued a handbill to deny that he had ever "spoken with intentional disrespect of religion."

Lincoln read the Bible extensively, and it provided him with major themes to interpret his presidency as well as the nation's history. In a speech to the New Jersey Senate in 1861, he said, "I shall be happy indeed if I shall be a humble instrument in the hands of the Almighty, and of this, his almost chosen people." Lincoln claimed to see in Scripture a basic understanding of the fundamental equality of all men in the sight of God. He argued that morality was rooted in religion and ultimately in the Bible, and was thus anchored in the will of God and not subject to human likes or dislikes.

A CIVIL WAR

Following Lincoln's election to the presidency, but before his inauguration could take place, the state of South Carolina proclaimed its withdrawal from the Union. Several proposals to drawn lines between slave territories and free territories were brought before Congress. When these failed, six more states seceded from the Union and, with South Carolina, combined to form the Confederate States of America. Fort Sumter was under siege. By the time Lincoln took office, the country was facing a major crisis.

War came and the bonds of affection were broken. Both Northern and Southern patriots identified their separate causes with the destiny of the nation. Both invoked the aid of the nation's God. Each viewed its own actions as defending the most fundamental principles of American government. Each assumed that its own military was the advance guard of the New Israel crossing the Red Sea of war to fulfill God's promise to the nation. Lincoln was one of the few public figures to rise above partisan interpretations of national purpose. As the divisions deepened and battles lengthened, Lincoln spoke of the war as a judgment on the whole nation. In response to a clergyman who expressed hope that God was on the side of the North, Lincoln had said that this did not worry him; rather, he was concerned that the North be on God's side.

Lincoln's overriding concern in his public speeches and correspondence seemed to be the preservation of the Union and its guarantee of democratic freedom. He write to Horace Greely that

> my paramount object in this struggle is to save the Union, and is not either to save or to destroy slavery. If I could save the Union without freeing any slave I would do it, and if I could save it by freeing all the slaves I would do it; and if I could do it by freeing some and leaving others alone I would also do that.

Lincoln argued that the preservation of the Union required fidelity to its divine origin as a nation conceived in liberty and dedicated to the proposition that all men are created equal. In the end, slavery stood in the way of union, and Lincoln, exercising the President's war powers, drafted an Emancipation Proclamation in the fall of 1862. In his annual message to Congress in December, he summarized his actions.

> In giving freedom to the slave, we assure freedom to the free—honorable alike in what we give and what we preserve. We shall nobly save, or meanly lose, the last, best hope of earth. . . . The way is plain, peaceful, generous, just—a way which, if followed, the world will forever applaud, and God must forever bless.

For Lincoln, it was the nation's destiny to beam forth rays of democratic freedom to the world, and this destiny was being tested by tragic war. Yet, as Lincoln vividly stated in his address at the dedication of the Gettysburg National Cemetery, the war might well prove the occasion for a renewed pledge to American destiny under God:

> It is for us, the living . . . to be here dedicated to the great task remaining before us—that from these honored dead we take increased devotion to that cause for which they gave the last full measure of devotion . . . that this nation, under God, shall have a new birth of freedom; and that government of the people, by the people, for the people, shall not perish from the earth.

SECOND INAUGURAL—4 MARCH 1865

Shouts rose from the crowd, and looking up, Joseph saw the Inaugural procession emerge from the eastern portico. High figures of all branches of government were present—Supreme Court Justices, members of the Senate, diplomats, heads of government departments, governors of states, and mayors of cities, and finally the President-elect. Lincoln took his place behind a small table with the members of the Supreme Court seated at his left and military guards below him facing the crowds. Then he rose and stepped forward, holding a large single sheet of paper in his hand. As he advanced to the table, a roar filled the air, and Joseph found himself joining vigorously in the repeated bursts of applause that swept the crowd like waves upon the shore, finally dying away on the outer fringes of the crowd. In the profound silence that followed, the clear and somewhat shrill tones of Lincoln's voice sounded over the vast concourse:

Fellow countrymen:

At this second appearing to take the oath of the presidential office, there is less occasion for an extended address than there was at the first. Then a statement, somewhat in detail of a course to be pursued, seemed fitting and proper. Now, at the expiration of four years, during which public declarations have been constantly called forth on every point and phase of the great contest which still absorbs the attention and engrosses the energies of the nation, little that is new could be presented. The progress of our arms, upon which all else chiefly depends, is as well-known to the public as to myself; and it is, I trust, reasonably satisfactory and encouraging to all. With high hope for the future, no prediction in regard to it is ventured.

On the occasion corresponding to this four years ago, all thoughts were anxiously directed to an impending civil war. All dreaded it—all sought to avert it. While the inaugural address was being delivered from this place, devoted altogether to saving the union without war, insurgent agents were in the city seeking to destroy it without war—seeking to dissolve the Union, and divide effects, by negotiation. Both parties deprecated war; but one of them would make war rather than let it perish. And the war came.

One-eighth of the whole population were colored slaves, not distributed generally over the Union, but localized in the Southern part of it. These slaves constituted a peculiar and powerful interest. All knew that this interest was, somehow, the cause of the war. To strengthen, perpetuate, and extend this interest was the object for which the insurgents would rend the Union, even by war; while the government claimed no right to do more than to restrict the territorial enlargement of it.

Neither party expected for the war the magnitude or the duration which

it has already attained. Neither anticipated that the cause of the conflict
might cease with, or even before, the conflict itself would cease. Each
looked for an easier triumph, and a result less fundamental and astounding.
Both read the same Bible, and pray to the same God; and each invokes his
aid against the other. It may seem strange that any men should dare to ask a
just God's assistance in wringing their bread from the sweat of other men's
faces; but let us judge not, that we be not judged. The prayers of both could
not be answered—that of neither has been answered fully.

The Almighty has his own purposes. "Woe unto the world because of
offenses! for it must needs be that offenses come; but woe to that man by
whom the offense cometh." If we shall suppose that American slavery is
one of those offenses which, in the providence of God, must needs come,
but which, having continued through his appointed time, he now wills to
remove, and that he gives to both North and South this terrible war, as the
woe due to those by whom the offense came, shall we discern therein any
departure from those divine attributes which the believers in a living God
always ascribe to him? Fondly do we hope—fervently do we pray—that
this mighty scourge of war may speedily pass away. Yet, if God wills that
it continue until all the wealth piled by the bondman's two hundred and
fifty years of unrequited toil shall be sunk, and until every drop of blood
drawn with the lash shall be paid by another drawn with the sword, as was
said three thousands years ago, so still it must be said, "The judgments of
the Lord are true and righteous altogether."

With malice toward none; with charity for all; with firmness in the
right, as God gives us to see the right, let us strive on to finish the work we
are in; to bind up the nation's wounds; to care for him who shall have borne
the battle, and for his widow, and his orphan—to do all which may achieve
and cherish a just and lasting peace among ourselves, and with all nations.

Joseph caught his breath. There it was, in phrase after ringing phrase
that mounted higher as if on eagle's wings. Blending words of the Old
Testament prophets and the Founding Fathers, Lincoln had again sur-
mounted the nation's differences. Slavery was a contradiction of God's
will and therefore the nation as a whole was subject to God's judgment.
North and South alike had profited from slavery and so judgment fell
alike on both sides, a "judgment that might continue until all the wealth
piled by the bondman's two hundred and fifty years of unrequited toil
shall be sunk. . . ." Yet, Joseph thought, if the war was a divine judgment upon the entire nation, it was judgment for a purpose: the renewal of
an America newly dedicated to an increase of freedom and justice: "with
malice toward none . . . with firmness in the right. . . ."

The prolonged cheers were coming to an end. Chief Justice Chase
directed the clerk of the Supreme Court to bring forward the Bible.
Lincoln, laying his right hand on the open Bible, repeated the oath of

office: "I do solemnly swear that I will faithfully execute the office of the President of the United States, and will, to the best of my ability, preserve, protect, and defend the Constitution of the United States—so help me God." Lincoln bent forward and kissed the book and then rose to his full height. The ceremony was complete. Abraham Lincoln was vested with the authority to serve an additional four years as President of the United States of America.

As he made his way back down Pennsylvania Avenue, Joseph reviewed the President's words, searching for new insight into the questions that still troubled him. The speech was filled with biblical allusions and references to Divine Sovereignty, and from Lincoln's mouth they had a ring of sincerity. Lincoln seemed to be religious, but not in the usual sense; how could he explain that in the article he was to write? What exactly was Lincoln's religion? Perhaps there would be opportunity for a question or two, he thought, as the White House came into view.

SELECTED BIBLIOGRAPHY

Abraham Lincoln

Basler, Roy P., ed. *The Collected Works of Abraham Lincoln.* 9 vols. New Brunswick, N.J.: 1953-55. Includes virtually all the known writings of Lincoln.

Sandburg, Carl. *Abraham Lincoln: The Prairie Years.* 2 vols. New York: Harcourt, Brace, 1926.

———. *Abraham Lincoln: The War Years.* 4 vols. New York: Harcourt, Brace, 1939.

Trueblood, Elton. *Abraham Lincoln: Theologian of American Anguish.* New York: Harper & Row, 1972.

Van Doren, Carl, ed. *The Literary Works of Abraham Lincoln.* New York: Heritage Press, 1942. A useful one-volume collection of Lincoln's more famous letters and speeches. See pp. 174-83, 216, 225-29, 255-57, 273-74.

Wolf, William J. *The Almost Chosen People.* Garden City, N.Y.: Doubleday, 1959. Rpt. as *The Religion of Abraham Lincoln.* New York: Seabury Press, 1963.

American Civil Religion

Bellah, Robert N. *The Broken Covenant: American Civil Religion in Time of Trial.* New York: Seabury Press, 1975.

Cherry, Conrad, ed. *God's New Israel.* Englewood Cliffs, N.J.: Prentice-Hall, 1971.

Mead, Sidney E. *The Lively Experiment.* New York: Harper & Row, 1963. See especially Mead's essay "Abraham Lincoln's 'Last, Best Hope of Earth': The American Dream of Destiny and Democracy," pp. 72-89.
———. *The Nation with the Soul of a Church.* New York: Harper & Row, 1975.
Richey, Russell E., and Donald G. Jones, eds. *American Civil Religion.* New York: Harper & Row, 1974.
Strout, Cushing. *The New Heavens and New Earth: Political Religion in America.* New York: Harper & Row, 1974.

The Emergence of Pentecostalism

This case was prepared by Donald W. Dayton

It was late in a sultry Missouri August in 1881 about six miles outside of St. Catherine in Linn County. A. M. Keirgan pondered the issues as he walked across the campground between a few of the nearly fifty tents and covered wagons to the one where the "workers" and organizers of the meeting were gathered to respond to an event that had the whole camp in an uproar. He had heard of similar events in other places, but he had been caught off guard when in the evening service, as he was to describe it later,

> right in the midst of a great sermon, a woman from Carroll County, a holiness professor, sprawled out at full length in the aisle. This, in itself, was not much to be thought of, for to tumble over now and then was to be expected. But the unexpected happened in this case. It kept some of the sisters busy to keep her with a measurable decent appearance. Directly she began to compose a jargon of words in rhyme and sing them with a weird tune. She persisted till the service was spoiled and the camp was thrown into a hubbub. Strange to say, the camp was divided thereby. Some said it was a wonderful manifestation of speaking in unknown tongues as at Pentecost. . . . [Others said it was of the devil.] But the camp was so divided in opinion that it had to be handled with the greatest of care.

The stance of the leadership would largely determine the response of those attending the camp meeting and would set the spiritual tone for the rest of the week. Was this experience a genuine work of the Spirit such that to suppress it would undercut the spiritual vitality that had been evident so far in the meeting? Or was this event a sidetrack or even a wile of the devil to draw attention away from the more appropriate emphasis on the conversion of sinners and the sanctification of believers? How should the camp workers respond to this strange event?

REVIVALISM AND THE RISE OF METHODISM

The issues had been simmering beneath the surface for at least a century in one form or another, especially in the circles impacted by the evangelical revival and the rise of Methodism. Intense spiritual struggles had been nurtured in the Puritan experience. And hearing the preaching of John Wesley, some were reported on occasion to have fallen to the ground under the conviction of sins and the power of the Spirit. By the 1770s Wesley had become less ambiguous in his teaching of a "second experience of grace" in which the believer entered a new level of Christian experience that Methodists were inclined to describe in terms of "Christian perfection" or "entire sanctification." Such an increasing emphasis on this point of "crisis" in Christian experience had even led to something of a theological fight with one of his closest coworkers, Anglican priest and theologian John Fletcher, who was inclined to see the account of Pentecost as a description of the "entire sanctification" of the disciples in a mighty "baptism of the Holy Spirit." Wesley had resisted that line of argument, fearing that the work of the Spirit in the Christian life would be inappropriately separated from conversion and justification. Under Wesley's influence Methodism tended to avoid the use of Pentecostal imagery to describe the "second blessing" but placed great emphasis on a direct "witness of the Spirit" in the heart of the believer that served as a form of spiritual "assurance" that, combined with a morally transformed life, provided "evidence" of conversion and sanctification.

But it was in the United States that Methodism had its great impact, growing from a handful of adherents at the time of the Revolution to the largest Protestant denomination by the Civil War. Combining with the theologically congenial currents flowing out of the great awakenings, Methodism gained force and set the tone for much of American Protestantism in the nineteenth century, giving shape in many ways to the "evangelical consensus" closely associated with the rise of revivalism—from the frontier revivals to the more sophisticated crusades in the major cities orchestrated by an emerging class of professional evangelicals.

Under Wesley, Methodism had had a special relationship to the lower classes, the workers, the miners, and so forth. With its success in America, Methodism became respectable, moved into the middle classes, began to establish seminaries, and took on the shape of the more established Congregational and Presbyterian churches in America. This led to great convulsions within Methodism and a process of fragmentation in which new churches and movements were formed, each claiming to preserve the original spirit of Methodism—its anti-slavery convictions (Wesleyan Church), its lay orientation (several groups early in the nineteenth century), its special relationship to the poor (the Free Methodist Church), and such practices as field preaching (the Salvation Army), and the Wesleyan teachings of "entire sanctification."

ENTIRE SANCTIFICATION

The teaching of entire sanctification was at the center of a "holiness revival" in the middle of the nineteenth century that had international impact and permeated most of the revivalism of the century. The Methodist sources of this revival included Phoebe Palmer, who led the widely imitated "Tuesday Meeting for the Promotion of Holiness" in New York City and edited the *Guide to Holiness,* and also the National Camp Meeting Association for the Promotion of Holiness which brought together Methodist evangelists with a special concern for the preaching of entire sanctification and found that the camp meeting was the best institution for keeping Methodism in touch with the masses. But, like the charismatic movement of the twentieth century, this search for a deeper Christian experience soon burst the bounds of Methodism to penetrate into Presbyterian, Congregationalist, Baptist, and other evangelical denominations—and became a major theme of the influential lay prayer revival of 1857-58. The great antebellum evangelist Charles Grandison Finney, though a Presbyterian, moved toward "holiness" teachings as well. In fact, we can trace the concerns for a deeper experience in the Christian faith through most of the revivalists of the century, especially D. L. Moody and his colaborers. These currents leapt the Atlantic and produced the Keswick movement among Anglicans, a more moderate holiness teaching that was reintroduced in the United States by Moody and became the semiofficial piety of the emerging fundamentalist/evangelical movement of the late nineteenth and early twentieth centuries.

The search for a deeper Christian experience was thus widespread in American culture and focused especially in those revivalistically oriented circles that were finding themselves increasingly embattled within a secularizing culture that was caught in the convulsions of modernity (urbanization, industrialization, pluralism, etc.). As the century came to a close the polarizations had become more profound. New sects and new denominations were being formed right and left. The fluidity and complexity of the situation provided the context in which new theological developments could easily take place.

Many groups and currents emerged that placed a special emphasis on the "restoration" of New Testament Christianity. This tendency was perhaps epitomized in the Campbellite movement that produced the Christian Church and the Churches of Christ, but at the very heart of revivalism itself was the concern to revive and restore the "primitive faith" or "piety." Increasingly the narrative of Pentecost came to the fore as the archetypal manifestation of the "apostolic faith" that seemed so vital and powerful and put to shame the anemic faith of the churches of the age. And within the holiness circles of Methodism this fascination with Pentecost again raised the old questions of John Fletcher about whether the disciples at Pentecost had experienced something like the "entire sanctification" of the Methodists that seemed to bring a spiritual power and clarity to modern lives caught in the upheaval of the times. Increasingly in the 1870s most conservative revivalists, whether radical camp meeting holiness preachers or the more refined Anglican and other established church members who had attended the Keswick Conferences, taught some form of a special second experience in the Holy Spirit that might be called an endowment of power or a "baptism of the Holy Spirit" along the model of Pentecost.

In the background of all this spiritual ferment was the question of "evidence." How might believers know that they were truly "saved" or "sanctified"—or living in God's will. The answers were various. Early Methodism had emphasized the "witness of the Spirit" and the evidence of a transformed life. Phoebe Palmer had argued basically against any evidence based in emotion or experience, but on occasion suggested that "testifying," or "prophesying," especially as moved by the Spirit, might constitute a sign of the "baptism." This experientially grounded search for an "evidence" or a form of tangible "assurance" was brought to the accounts of the book of Acts, and it was only a matter of time before the proposal would emerge that the evidence of being baptized in the Spirit was the gift of "speaking in an unknown tongue as at Pentecost."

THE EMERGENCE OF PENTECOSTALISM

A. M. Keirgan could have been only subliminally aware of all the historical and theological currents that were finding focus in the Missouri camp meeting that night—or the fact that this situation would repeat itself many times during the last third of the nineteenth century. He could not know that he was laying the foundation for the emergence of a small holiness denomination that would later be known as the Churches of God, or more commonly the Independent Holiness People. As a Methodist minister he had come under the influence of the holiness teachings in late 1875, attracted by the spiritual vitality of its advocates. Within a couple of years he was opening up his church to "holiness conventions," an act that led eventually to his removal from the charge. This repudiation by the church hierarchy led to his being increasingly marginalized within the Methodist system and to an accompanying attraction to a radical ecclesiology that promised an end to denominationalism by the restoration of primitive Christianity. Before the end of the decade, Keirgan had become an independent holiness evangelist, circulating among the churches and camp meetings of Missouri.

The camp meeting just north of St. Catherine was pitched on clay hills in a community of the poor. There was already a community of perhaps fifty converts to the holiness message, forty of them the product of a split within the local Baptist church. People had come from several counties to hear the preaching of holiness evangelists prominent in the Midwest. The preaching had been, in Keirgan's words, "unctious and powerful," and the "altar services . . . were times of much weeping and rejoicing." The "converted" and the "sanctified" came into each "service all prayed up and all melted and wet with the dews of grace and ready for a renewed attack on the kingdom of darkness."

And just when the meeting was "in fine swing and the tide was high," this strange event had occurred. How should the leadership respond? Was this a new spiritual experience that should be cultivated? Or was it a work of the devil to destroy the vitality of the camp and lead the people into a blind alley? Little did A. M. Keirgan realize that he was witnessing a rebirth of Pentecostalism, destined to become one of the most powerful religious forces of the twentieth century. Little did he realize that the questions he faced that night would emerge again and again over the next century until all Christendom would be struggling with his questions.

SELECTED BIBLIOGRAPHY

The incident described in this case is reported by A. M. Keirgan in *Historical Sketches of the Revival of True Holiness and Local Church Polity, 1865-1916,* an informal 1972 reprint of articles that originally appeared in various issues of *The Church Advocate and Good Way,* early in this century.

Anderson, Robert Mapes. *The Vision of the Disinherited: The Making of American Pentecostalism.* New York: Oxford University Press, 1979.

Dayton, Donald W., ed. *The Higher Christian Life: Sources for the Study of the Holiness, Pentecostal, and Keswick Movements.* 48 vols. New York: Garland, 1984-86.

————. *Theological Roots of Pentecostalism.* Metuchen, N.J.: Scarecrow Press, 1986.

Hollenweger, Walter J. *The Pentecostals: The Charismatic Movement in the Churches.* Minneapolis: Augsburg, 1972.

Synan, H. Vinson. *The Holiness-Pentecostal Movement in the United States.* Grand Rapids: Eerdmans, 1971.

James Cardinal Gibbons and the Americanization of the Catholic Church

This case was prepared by Louis B. Weeks

Fall 1893, and James Cardinal Gibbons prepared his prayers for the World Parliament of Religions in Chicago. Here Hindus, Buddhists, Moslems, and Christians would meet and discuss beliefs and religious practice with each other. Gibbons had been sought out to deliver opening and closing prayers, while his colleagues Bishops Ireland and Keane would present papers. This was an opportunity for Gibbons to present Roman Catholicism as compatible with American social and political life. At the same time, he worried that his apparent tolerance for other religious views would be interpreted as another evidence that American Catholics no longer honored the pope and the traditional faith. The battle had been a long and difficult one, with Gibbons frequently at the center of controversy. Now, however, he might show how human belief was unified and how Catholicism need not be defensive in a pluralistic environment. Gibbons prayed about his blessing and prayers.

JAMES GIBBONS, PRIEST

Born in Baltimore, Maryland, in 1834, James Gibbons was the fourth child and first son of Thomas and Bridget Gibbons, recent immigrants from Ireland. James grew up first in America, then in Ballinrobe, Ireland, where his family returned because of his father's poor health. After his father's death, James returned to the United States with his mother to live in New Orleans.

After surviving a serious bout with yellow fever, and influenced by Redemptorist priests, especially Father John Duffy, Gibbons had decided to become a priest. Gibbons studied at a Sulpician minor seminary in

Baltimore, and at St. Mary's Seminary, also under that order. He was ordained in 1861, and he served as an assistant pastor at St. Patrick's Church, Fell's Point, and as a pastor of two mission churches nearby. He served as volunteer chaplain for Forts Marshall and McHenry nearby.

In June 1865, Martin J. Spalding, Archbishop of Baltimore, assigned Gibbons as his own episcopal secretary. Soon afterward, he recommended Gibbons to the Vatican to become bishop of North Carolina. In 1868, at the age of thirty-three, he was consecrated—the youngest Roman Catholic bishop in the world at the time.

At the time of Gibbons's assignment to the Diocese of North Carolina, it was almost nonexistent—three priests serving a few congregations and a small stucco "cathedral" in Wilmington with a lean-to for a residence. Hard work helped improve the situation by the time Gibbons moved to become bishop of Richmond in 1872. He remained in charge of North Carolina as well.

Gibbons continued to rise in the American hierarchy. In 1877, he was appointed coadjutor to the Archbishop of Baltimore, James Roosevelt Bayley, who had succeeded Spalding in 1872. When Bayley died, Gibbons was Archbishop of America's premier see. He became a cardinal in 1886. For many years, he served as a kind of embodiment of American Catholicism, loyal to the Church while eager to defend American politics and values.

ROMAN CATHOLICS IN AMERICA

While in Richmond, Gibbons had composed a concise statement of Catholic doctrine and practice for American consumption entitled *The Faith of Our Fathers*. The work set forth many of the Church's teachings, buttressed liberally with quotations from Scripture that would help Protestants and the unchurched see biblical authority for Catholic practice. The book sold quickly, and it helped many Americans understand their Roman Catholic neighbors.

Understanding had not usually characterized the relationship of Protestants to Catholics in America. Colonial laws had discriminated against Catholics in the areas of business and politics, even sometimes in Maryland where freedom had usually prevailed. The fact that Catholicism prevailed in almost all of Latin America did not help matters at all.

In the new United States, most Protestants had taken for granted the close relationship of politics and denominationalism. They had espoused thorough and sometimes virulent anti-Roman sentiments. Especially as

Irish Catholics began to immigrate in large numbers, "nativism" grew as a movement to oppose their bids for incorporation into American common life. Fully one million had arrived in the United States between 1815 and 1845, and the arrival of still more threatened the tenuous social fabric in the cities where they settled. And in addition to the Irish, Catholics from Italy, Germany, and various other countries also came to America in large numbers. By the time of the Civil War, there were more Catholics in America than Protestants of any single denomination.

Roman Catholic leaders in Europe did little to help the cause of these people. Immigrants were not prepared to accept the validity of other religious perspectives. Vatican spokesmen intimated that American Catholics should take over political power where possible, establish true "Christian" schools, and convert the wayward non-Catholics. Parochial schools were established by Catholics, and Catholic "ghettos" of sorts grew in the cities in parishes of various ethnic groups.

KNOW NOTHINGS AND AMERICANISTS

Anti-Catholic sentiments flourished among Protestants in the early 1900s, but they became even more broadly based in political groups. In the 1850s, the cry of "No Papacy," which had sporadically seized Protestant imaginations, became the rallying cry of the "Know-Nothings," a movement centered in but not limited to the American Party. Many states, both slave and free, elected especially "anti-Catholic" legislatures that year. American Party candidates succeeded in winning seventy-five seats in the congressional elections of 1854. Had the new Republican Party not also fared well in 1856, and had the slavery-abolition issue not split the American Party decisively that year, the Know-Nothings might have done even better in the next election.

At the same time, American Catholicism gained in stature with some able leaders among the American hierarchy and with some famous converts touting the faith. Especially important were the models of Isaac Hecker and Orestes Brownson, New England intellectual leaders who became Roman Catholic in adulthood and who advocated American tolerance of the faith (and, indeed, American conversion to it). Hecker, converted in 1844, later founded the Paulist order, a specific religious congregation dedicated to mission among American non-Catholics. Brownson, much older than Hecker, also converted in 1844, and he subsequently published pro-Catholic apologetics in his *Brownson's Quarterly Review*.

Brownson advocated "Americanism" for the Catholic Church in the United States, adoption of its system and authority structure to the voluntary and independent environment of the New World. He claimed the tradition of John Carroll, the first American bishop, for his own. Hecker, too, advocated Roman flexibility, especially in relating to the American political and religious environment.

Rome, meanwhile, was undergoing enormous pressures and vicissitudes. Pope Pius IX responded by promulgating a Syllabus of Errors in 1864, a militant defense of the church against modern incursions. The ecumenical council of 1869-70, affirming the doctrine of papal infallibility, added to the controversy.

The three most outspoken proponents of Americanism among American Catholic leaders in the 1880s were John Ireland, archbishop of Saint Paul; John Keane, bishop of Richmond; and Denis O'Connell, rector first of the first North American College in Rome and then of Catholic University. Gibbons was seen as an Americanist also, though not so partisan a proponent in matters of dispute.

Ireland fought establishment of semiautonomous monastic communities (especially within his own diocese), and he and Americanist colleagues generally opposed the use of languages other than English for instruction in parochial schools. Many of the Americanists advocated temperance measures and restrictions against distilleries and breweries. And the Americanists advocated the establishment of an American Catholic University so that future leaders would not have to go to Europe to receive a higher education.

Americanists generally supported labor movements, in contrast to the traditional Vatican stance of opposing all organizations with such aims as labor had. The Knights of Labor, a major Catholic-oriented organization, moreover, held secret meetings and possessed rituals that prompted Roman authorities to condemn them. Gibbons interceded to prevent Vatican condemnation and to assure Rome the objectionable practices had ceased.

THE WORLD PARLIAMENT OF RELIGIONS

Gibbons served as a member of the auxiliary that sought to organize meetings of world leaders from various fields of endeavor in conjunction with the Columbian Exposition, popularly known as the Chicago World Fair, which began in 1893. He also became honorary president of the American Catholic Congress, one of those gatherings. That meeting in

September of 1893 provided a setting for the Vatican representative to praise American Catholics. He served in both capacities without receiving any criticism or hostile reaction.

However, in participating in the Parliament, Gibbons opened the possibility of conflict. For one thing, John Ireland and John Keane, two bishops thoroughly identified with Americanism, were also reading papers. In addition, perhaps more importantly, in blessing the Parliament he might seem to be recognizing all religions as equally valid, as alternatives equally acceptable before God—a position the Roman Catholic church repudiated. Protestants and "fallen away Catholics" were enough in error. Hindus, Moslems, and Buddhists? Well, that was too much!

In proposing Roman Catholic participation in the Parliament, John Keane had emphasized that it was an exposition, a display of various religions, and not a debate or discussion as to which was the true one or even better than others. Keane thought quite naturally that Gibbons should accept the honor and lead the effort. But Gibbons had initially hesitated. Once accepting the task, though, the priest wondered what to pray.

SELECTED BIBLIOGRAPHY

Ellis, John T. *The Life of James Cardinal Gibbons, Archbishop of Baltimore, 1834-1921.* 2 vols. Milwaukee: Bruce Publishing, 1952.

Gibbons, James Cardinal. *A Retrospect of Fifty Years.* 2 vols. Baltimore: John Murphy, 1916.

Leckie, Robert. *American and Catholic.* Garden City, N.Y.: Doubleday, 1970.

McAvoy, Thomas. *The Great Crisis in American Catholic History, 1895-1900.* Chicago: Regnery, 1957.

Tehan, John, and Arline Boucher. *Prince of Democracy: James Cardinal Gibbons.* New York: Image Books, 1966.

Walter Rauschenbusch and the Social Awakening of the Churches

This case was prepared by Donald K. Gorrell

When Walter Rauschenbusch sent the completed manuscript of his book *Christianizing the Social Order* to the Macmillan Company in October 1912, he felt more confident than he had when he submitted the text of his first book in 1906. His life was changed by the publication of that first book, *Christianity and the Social Crisis,* in 1907. He was catapulted from relative obscurity to national fame. Thereafter Rauschenbusch stood in the front rank of Social Gospel leaders. As he recognized afterward, "The social movement had got hold of me, just as the social awakening was getting hold of the country. The book came out at the psychological moment, and was taken as an expression of what thousands were feeling." In the years that followed he was in constant demand as a lecturer and consultant, and the public was now ready to receive another book from the acknowledged spokesman for social Christianity.

THE LONELY PROPHET

While fame came suddenly, the ideas Rauschenbusch expressed had been part of his thinking for many years. He was forty-six years old in 1907, but his notoriety had begun when he was twenty-five, when he had assumed the pastorate of the Second German Baptist Church in the poor, working-class section of New York City known as Hell's Kitchen. His pious, classical education in the home of an immigrant German Baptist preacher and in schools in Germany and Rochester had not prepared him for ministry to the needs of the people. Gradually he acquired social information and developed a social passion, but not without difficulties.

"The church held down the social interest in me. It contradicted it; it opposed it; it held it down as far as it could; and when it was a question about giving me position or preferment, the fact that I was interested in the workingman was actually against me—not for me." During his New York ministry (1886-97) he caught influenza in a blizzard and the after-effects left him deaf the rest of his life. His social ideas developed amid this physical and ecclesiastical loneliness, but he neither lost his optimistic faith nor lost contact with the small group of people who were working with similar ideas and values. In 1897 he became professor of New Testament interpretation in the German department of Rochester Theological Seminary, and from 1902 until his death in 1918 he was professor of church history at the seminary.

Enjoying the stimulation and fellowship of groups concerned with the relation of religion to society, Rauschenbusch participated in the Baptist Congress, the New York State Conference of Religion, and the Religious Education Association. His group with which he was primarily involved, however, was the Brotherhood of the Kingdom, which he helped to establish in 1893. At these various associations he sometimes presented papers expressing his germinal thoughts, but he had published no major work before *Christianity and the Social Crisis,* and he was not well-known outside a small circle.

CHRISTIANITY AND THE SOCIAL CRISIS

He began to write his "epoch-making work" three times in fifteen years before his social passion about economic, political, and social events in 1905-06 finally enabled him to transform a pedestrian, schol-arly initial text into a vibrant social message. "I wrote the book with a lot of fear and trembling," he said. "I expected there would be a good deal of anger and resentment." Hoping to miss the worst of the anticipated reaction, he took a year's sabbatical leave in Germany shortly after the book was published. To his astonishment the book was favorably re-ceived in 1907, and by 1912 had run through over a dozen big editions, which put it in a class equalled by only a few best-selling novels of the time.

A vivid chapter entitled "The Present Crisis" contained a strong indictment of American society; he went on to argue that "the crisis of society is also the crisis of the Church." The church had three choices as he saw it: to withdraw from the evil world, "to tolerate the world and conform to it," or "to condemn the world and seek to change it." He maintained that the third option was the only realistic one: it was necessary that the church stimulate the moral forces against wrong. "The fighting energy of those moral forces will . . . depend on the degree to which they are inspired by religious faith and enthusiasm. It is either a revival of religion or the deluge."

THE SOCIAL AWAKENING OF THE CHURCHES

A series of actions and responses by the Protestant churches in the years after his first book led Rauschenbusch to feel that the long-awaited revival of religion had begun. Through the combined reforming energies of the Progressive Movement and the journalistic disclosures of the Muckrakers, a social awakening was taking place outside the churches. Within Protestantism a "Social Creed of the Churches" was adopted in 1908 by the newly established Federal Council of the Churches of Christ in America. And during 1911-12 a great evangelism effort known as the Men and Religion Forward Movement aroused the interest and response of thousands. As he shared in these movements, Rauschenbusch believed that his deeply felt social concerns were being implemented and he sought to convince others that "within recent years we have witnessed a strange revival of Christianity, a social awakening of the church."

"CHRISTIANIZING THE SOCIAL ORDER"

In that changing situation various constituencies encouraged Rauschenbusch to write another book, and his publishers were certainly eager for him to do so. He had delivered two series of lectures on the theme "Christianizing the Social Order," and he proposed a book of that title to his editor, which he briefly described in this way:

> "Christianizing the Social Order" is to take up the question where "Christianity and the Social Crisis" stopped. The former book called for a social awakening of the moral and religious forces: the new book will show that this awakening is now taking place, and to that extent is full of hopefulness. It will examine the present social order to determine what portions have not yet submitted to the revolutionizing influences of the Christian law and spirit. The process by which these unredeemed sections of modern life can be christianized will be discussed. It will exhibit a Christian Social Order in the process of making. The closing chapter will show that in performing this great task, religion itself will be rejuvenated and increasingly christianized.

Teaching and speaking obligations delayed the completion of the book until October 1912, despite pleas from the publishers. *Christianizing the Social Order* reached book stores 20 November 1912, just after the Progressive Era had reached its peak in Theodore Roosevelt's unsuccessful "Bull Moose" presidential campaign against Woodrow Wilson and William Howard Taft.

In its final form, *Christianizing the Social Order* consisted of six major parts. In the first, with the eyes of an historian as well as the judgment of a social prophet, Rauschenbusch's survey of the contemporary social awakening of the churches provided an insider's view of the events of the preceding decade. The second part sought "to show that the christianizing of the social order was the very aim with which Christianity set out." Part three subjected the "present social order to a moral analysis in order to determine what is Christian in the structure, and what is not." Here he concluded that the Family, Church, Education, and Political Life were christianized but that the Economic Order was not. In part four Rauschenbusch showed that "the unregenerate elements of our social organization are not quietly waiting till we get ready to reform them, but are actively invading God's country and devastating the moral achievements built up by centuries of Christian teaching and sacrifice." The fifth part traced the basic lines of moral evolution needed to institutionalize Christian convictions. And part six suggested the methods of personal and social action "by which our present conditions can be molded into a juster and happier community life in which the Christian spirit shall be more free to work its will."

As he ended his foreword and turned the book over to the reader, Rauschenbusch indicated the motive, purpose, and tone he intended:

> If this book were to be written at all, it had to deal searchingly with the great collective sins of our age. Evangelism always seeks to create a fresh conviction of guilt as a basis for a higher righteousness, and this book is nothing if it is not a message of sin and salvation. But its purpose is not denunciation. It is wholly constructive. Of "Christianity and the Social Crisis" it has been said that it is a book without any hate in it. So far as I know my own soul that is true of this book, too. I have written it as a follower of Jesus Christ. My sole desire has been to summon the Christian passion of justice and the Christian powers of love and mercy to do their share in redeeming our social order from its inherent wrongs.

SELECTED BIBLIOGRAPHY

Handy, Robert T. *The Social Gospel in America, 1870-1920*. New York: Oxford University Press, 1966.

Hopkins, C. Howard. *The Rise of the Social Gospel in American Protestantism, 1865-1915*. New Haven: Yale University Press, 1940.

Rauschenbusch, Walter. *Christianity and the Social Crisis*. New York: Macmillan, 1907.

————. *Christianizing the Social Order*. New York: Macmillan, 1912.

————. *A Theology for the Social Gospel*. New York: Macmillan, 1917.

Sharpe, Dores R. *Walter Rauschenbusch*. New York: Macmillan, 1942.

White, Ronald C., Jr., and C. Howard Hopkins. *The Social Gospel: Religion and Reform in Changing America*. Philadelphia: Temple University Press, 1976.

Part Four
Toward Pluralism

In the middle and latter decades of the twentieth century, American Christianity has continued its fascinating development. Trends from previous periods have continued to characterize the religious environment. Much of the theology in the leaders of America has still come from Europe, but much of the organization and religious practice remains distinctly American. Religious toleration has grown to the point that it can be argued that the nature of American religious pluralism has in fact changed. And the churches, at least most of them, show signs of maturity, as though American Christianity has finally grown up.

Among the trends from previous periods that have continued are the emphases on revivalism, on Christian "fundamentals," on social action, and on maintenance of distinct religious traditions. Aimee Semple McPherson, the first nationally prominent woman revivalist, led Californians especially with her Foursquare Gospel. Father Divine, a black preacher, also gathered Christians in the tradition of revivalistic communitarianism. Billy Sunday, who began even before McPherson, called America to the altar time and again, working city after city in behalf of local sponsors. In the decades after World War II, Billy Graham has led a host of revivalists in preaching for conversion and rededication, pioneering in the use of radio, television, movies, and other media to further his efforts. His friendship with presidents of corporations and leaders of nations has given revivalism a respectability it never had before, at least since Charles G. Finney's time. His efforts went beyond those of his predecessors in encouraging worldwide evangelization by an increasing band of itinerant evangelists, by far the greatest number at work in the Third World.

Fundamentalism has continued unabated as well, frequently accompanying the revivals and undergirding them. William Jennings Bryan, though declining in health and mental acuity by the time of the Scopes trial, still represented the views of a great many Americans as he condemned teaching that seemed to undercut doctrines of creation and providence. Similarly fierce defenses of Christian doctrines of the virgin birth of Christ and bodily resurrection have continued from many quarters.

Revivalists have not been altogether removed from the social implications of the gospel. Billy Sunday railed against drinkers and sellers of spirits. Billy Graham has accentuated honesty, marital fidelity, and other "mundane" values. But many Christians in the United States have involved themselves in movements deeper than prohibition and more specific than calls to be honest and faithful—movements to bring the gospel to bear in all the human condition. Harry Emerson Fosdick led the way, along with the advocates of the Social Gospel. Fosdick said that Christ's coming meant that "his will and principles will be worked out by God's grace in human life and institutions." A. J. Muste, pastor of the Labor Temple in New York, identified with working people. Dorothy Day, with her *Catholic Worker,* interpreted socialism for Americans in a Roman Catholic vocabulary. All these and many other Christians sought to inculcate the message of Scripture in the idiom of American social life.

The most obvious recipient of the spirit of the Social Gospel, however, has been the American civil rights movement. American Christianity gave birth to this movement, whether one chooses to date its beginnings to the time of the founding of the National Association for the Advancement of Colored People in 1909, to the ascendancy of Adam Clayton Powell in Harlem in the 1940s, or to the Montgomery bus boycott in 1954. W. E. B. DuBois made the connection in his analysis of the black church, and there was clearly a significant Christian presence, both preachers and laity, among his coworkers in the N.A.A.C.P. Adam Clayton Powell, who spurred the government to integrate the Armed Forces and led other protests against Jim Crowism, centered his political power in the Abyssinian Baptist Church, where he ministered. And Rosa Parks's action in refusing to yield a seat in a bus to a white man consolidated black church support for the struggle against racism in American life.

Martin Luther King, Jr., probably the foremost Christian personality in America in the twentieth century, led the civil rights movement in such a manner as to assemble a broad coalition of people of good will, black and white, rich and poor, Christian and non-Christian, educated and illiterate. And as the black church changed the civil rights movement, so the civil rights movement changed the black church. During the 1950s, black pastors and their congregations in America increased their emphasis on the "this-worldly" needs of their people. Black churches became centers for anti-poverty work, for rallies to register voters, and for religious activities designed to change society in other ways. Predominantly white churches learned from black churches and in some cases moved to institute many of the same kinds of services.

Different communions have also acted to preserve their distinct religious traditions. This effort is most evident among Eastern Orthodox churches and groups whose ethnicity is bound to their religious observance. Armenian Orthodox churches in the United States, for example, continue to celebrate worship in a liturgy that condemns all "biphysites"—those who profess that Christ had two distinct natures, human and divine. Of course virtually all American Christians are biphysites, and they reject monophysitism as heretical. But few on either side of the issue are consciously aware that the controversy surrounding it dates all the way back to the Council of Nicea in A.D. 325. Indeed, in the context of American religious life, few on either side raise the issue at all. Armenian Orthodox are regularly welcomed to participate in ecumenical endeavors, and they offer "portions" (blessed bread) for all who worship with them, regardless of their Christology. But the traditions continue.

Much of the theology of American religion has come from Europe. Karl Barth has been the most influential theologian for the contemporary mainstream churches. His neo-orthodoxy held sway for several decades and still influences thought in some denominations. Barth, a Swiss pastor and later a professor at the University of Basel, accentuated the difference between God and humanity. He offered the Bible as a qualitatively different authority from other books, as "The Word of God." He spoke of God's transcendence, of Christ as God's incarnation, and of the Christian life as discipleship more than as social amelioration. Emil Brunner, too, called for a reinvestment of the Christian in classic theology.

The life and death of Dietrich Bonhoeffer lent a stamp of authenticity to the neo-orthodox Christianity of the continent, although Bonhoeffer's theology differed in many respects from Barth's. Bonhoeffer wrote *Letters and Papers from Prison* and finally suffered a martyr's death resisting the regime of Adolph Hitler in Germany.

Rudolph Bultmann threatened the facile among American Christians who bothered to read his works. He stressed the radical nature of the call to follow Christ, and he also questioned the factuality of biblical "events." His efforts to "demythologize" the biblical narratives, especially those relating to the life and work of Christ, drew hostile charges from some that he was seeking to undercut the authority of Scripture with his criticism. Other Americans, however, rejoiced to be led through simple affirmation of biblical accounts to simple declarations concerning the nature of the faith.

The convening of Vatican II by Pope John XXIII invited fresh winds of renewal to sweep through the Roman Catholic Church, including the American Church. Since the days of Cardinal Gibbons, American Catholics had had to deal with the tension between received Catholic tradition and the particular values and institutions of American culture. At Vatican II this tension manifested itself in a variety of issues, especially the American tradition of religious freedom as it was interpreted by the Jesuit theologian John Courtney Murray.

If its theology has remained deeply indebted to European thought, American Christianity has nevertheless shown a willingness to experiment with new liturgical forms, theological education, and other aspects of Christian practice. The recognition that pastors should be trained professionally has led the American denominations to follow new developments for education in other professions; many seminaries now supplement traditional ministerial training programs with experientially based, work-related, inductively focused curricula. The use of nontraditional musical instruments in worship, expressions in dance, dialogue sermons, and house church patterns have been far more prevalent in the United States than on the Continent.

American-born theologians have moved to challenge the thoughts of the Europeans also. Reinhold Niebuhr, skillful and pragmatic, may have provided theological underpinnings for our national policy in politics during the Eisenhower years. Both Secretary of State John Foster Dulles and the first architect of America's "containment policy" toward Russia, George Kennan, read and followed Niebuhr's publications and sought his advice on matters of state. Niebuhr's *Moral Man and Immoral Society* bent neo-orthodox theology to the study of ethics and Christian decision making for generations of ministers and informed laypeople. And his sense of balance helped Christians think through the lives they led, the faith they followed.

Most American Christians in the second half of the twentieth century would probably deny that they had become pluralistic, except in the limited meaning of that word—"tolerant." But the fact is that most Americans—and most American religious bodies—have become a good deal more pluralistic over time. The coexistence of distinct ethnic, religious, and cultural groups, has long been a mark of American life, especially in the wake of King's vigorous and successful efforts in the national civil rights movement, with its ethical focus on housing patterns, job discrimination, and educational institutions. But pluralism at a more profound level has become a dominant mark in American Christianity— pluralism in the sense of a belief that reality is composed of many ulti- mately different substances, that no single theology or philosophy can account for everything in the whole world. Many American Catholics, Protestants, and Orthodox now believe in the value of ecumenical Chris- tianity, understanding the Christian faith to allow multivariate patterns of living and communing.

Pluralism is obvious in the new patterns of behavior we have accepted and adopted—a Baptist reading a horoscope, a Presbyterian knocking on wood for good luck, a Catholic dissenting from the Church's stand prohibiting birth control (a "matter of faith and morals"), an Orthodox Christian studying yoga. On every hand, in matters profound and frivo- lous, there is evidence pointing to believers' dependence on divergent sources of authority and religious vitality—evidence of profound pluralism.

Americans have for the most part been pluralistic all along in matters of religious toleration, although there was admittedly some active dis- crimination by Christians toward those who professed other religions— Buddhists, Muslims, Hindus, Jews—earlier in the nation's history. But this discrimination has now largely disappeared. The most notable change has occurred with regard to Judaism. Only sects still work to convert Jews to Christianity in some organized fashion. Though anti- Semitism can be discerned among Christians still, most American churches are aware that their religious roots are in Judaism and consider their religious life to be enriched by the presence of the Jewish communi- ty in the United States.

The Jewish population in the United States had been small until the latter years of the nineteenth century, but between 1870 and 1920 at least two million Jews immigrated. On the whole these new Americans did not embrace Reform Judaism, which had permeated the new country, em- phasizing commonality with Christianity more than distinctiveness in language and religious worldview. The new immigrants retained at least remnants of the Eastern European culture with its Yiddish expressions and orthodox observances. In response to anti-Semitism, new Jewish peoples in America grew in solidarity through Zionism, a fervent hope organized first in Europe to inhabit a modern Jewish State in Palestine.

Within Judaism itself, a spectrum of American organizations emerged. American Christians responded in a variety of ways to this new American Judaism. Some actively anti-Semitic Christians voiced their negative feelings in words and terrorism. A few denominations still seek mass conversions of Jews as a sign of the eschaton, and they relish reports from Hebrew Christians who evangelize toward that end. Most Christians, however, send Sunday School classes to synagogues to learn and participate with Jewish organizations in ecumenical endeavors. Some Christians even observe *sedarim* (sedar meals) and look to the bar mitzvah tradition to interpret the meaning of Christian confirmation.

What is true of interreligious pluralism is also true of intra-Christian relations. Not a few believers have come to discover that they are more critical of their own denomination than they are of other portions of the Christian family. This sort of situation can lead to a kind of "religious schizophrenia," to a split between denominational loyalties and ecumenical loyalties. But more characteristically, members of American religious mainstream traditions cooperate thoroughly in providing social services and interdenominational services. Through the Consultation on Christian Union, several even explore integral union among Protestant denominations.

Not all the denominations are open to each other, however. A number of sects, and some more established churches refuse to honor any pluralism—Jehovah's Witnesses, for example, and the Church of Jesus Christ of the Latter Day Saints (Mormons). Overall, however, there is increasingly a pluralistic understanding of the place of particular heritages among the Christian family.

John Scopes and the Debate over Evolution

This case was prepared by Jack Rogers, utilizing in part a previously unpublished case by students under his supervision: Bruce Norquist, Kurt Stephan, and David Lux.

John Scopes slumped at the defense table under the shade of trees on the courthouse lawn. For a few days, Dayton, Tennessee, had been the focus of national attention. It was Tuesday morning, 21 July 1925. Two thousand people were milling about excitedly following Judge John Raulston's declaration that the jury had found Scopes guilty. He had never imagined that his admitted disobedience to the Butler Act would have such far-reaching implications. Scopes mused that he had taken a back seat to other personalities and deeper issues. What ordinarily would have been a simple misdemeanor trial had assumed gigantic proportions as William Jennings Bryan argued for a literally interpreted Bible and against the agnosticism of Clarence Darrow. Had Christianity really been on trial? Was the validity of science being judged? Or were people simply confused?

AMERICA IN THE EARLY TWENTIETH CENTURY

The United States had recently emerged from a "war to end all wars." The rapid shift from rural to urban society brought both prosperity and problems. Immigration rates spiraled, and the nation emerged from international isolationism into an expansionist attitude marked by a sense of "manifest destiny." These vast changes elicited reactions on all hands.

In politics, a populist uprising was fashioned into progressivism. In religion, literary criticism of the Bible fueled the growth of theological liberalism. Some feared new international involvements and further immigration. They blamed the "German barbarism" of World War I on the

Darwinian philosophy of "survival of the fittest." In 1919 a group of theologically conservative Christians concerned about biblical criticism formed the interdenominational World's Christian Fundamentals Association (WCFA), calling for an exorcism of modernism and all its associated demons—especially evolutionism.

EVENTS LEADING TO THE TRIAL

In the spring of 1925, an obscure legislator in the Tennessee House of Representatives, John Washington Butler, introduced a measure prohibiting the teaching of evolution in the public schools and universities of the state. A lecture of William Jennings Bryan entitled "Is the Bible True?" had been distributed to the members of the legislature while the bill was being considered. The bill passed both houses of the legislature and was signed by the governor, who indicated that he had no intention of enforcing it. A political act popular with the voters of Tennessee led to a famous trial when the American Civil Liberties Union (ACLU) advertised that it would finance a test case to challenge the constitutionality of the law. A New York–educated mining engineer, George Rappelyea, living in Dayton, Tennessee, persuaded a young biology teacher in that town to be the defendant in such a case. Rappelyea swore out a warrant against Scopes, who was then arrested. Local businessmen didn't want their neighboring city of Chattanooga to be the cite of the first test case, so John T. Raulston, a circuit judge and lay preacher from Gizzards Cove, hastily called a special session of the Grand Jury. The jury returned an indictment, and Raulston ordered a special term of court for 10 July to try Scopes.

The trial gained widespread attention when the WCFA asked William Jennings Bryan to assist the prosecution. This raised the ire of Clarence Darrow, an agnostic and the most famous criminal lawyer in America. Darrow volunteered his services without fee to the defense. Both the local prosecution and the ACLU were somewhat dubious about the celebrated volunteer help they were receiving. But in the end, both sides were pressured to proceed with these famous participants.

LEADERS FOR THE DEFENSE AND PROSECUTION

Bryan had been a lawyer, editor of a newspaper called *The Commoner,* congressman from Nebraska, and three times unsuccessful candidate for President of the United States on the Democratic ticket. He was a highly popular, inspirational orator on the Chautauqua lecture circuit and a Presbyterian elder deeply emersed in the church struggles over biblical criticism and modernism. He had served as Secretary of State under Woodrow Wilson but resigned because of his conviction that the United States should remain neutral and act as arbiter rather than be participant in a European war. Bryan believed that Social Darwinism, transmitted through the writings of Nietzsche, was the cause of German aggression.

Clarence Darrow had defended more than fifty individuals charged with first-degree murder and lost only one client, his first, to execution. He also gained national fame through a series of labor trials including the defense of Socialist Eugene Debs and a splinter group of the Communist Labor Party. His defense of the teenage killers Leopold and Loeb established his reputation as "attorney for the damned." Politically, Darrow supported the radical ideas of the period, advocating a welfare state, abolition of monopolies, and organized labor. He supported Bryan in his 1896 and 1900 presidential bids but later favored the Socialist Party. In Darrow's view the job of the state was to protect freedom of self-expression. Any limitation of freedom, whether it involved prohibition of liquor, limitation of free speech, or teaching of evolution in the schools was an abomination to him. Darrow declared himself an agnostic and despised what he took to be Christian dogmatism.

THE TRIAL

Friday, the tenth of July, a carnival atmosphere descended on Dayton, Tennessee. Decorations and balloons festooned the main street and hot dog and watermelon stands sprouted on every corner. Dayton's normal population of 1,500 was swollen to twice that size.

At the courthouse, Judge Raulston discovered that Attorney General Stewart questioned the legality of the hastily drawn indictment. Raulston quickly empaneled a new Grand Jury. By 11:00 A.M. a new indictment was returned and *Tennessee v. John Thomas Scopes* was officially underway.

Testimony began the following Monday. The proceedings were somewhat delayed so that electrical engineers could finish hooking up connections for the first radio broadcast trial in history. Raulston proudly announced: "My gavel will be heard around the world."

The defense first moved to quash the indictment on the grounds that it violated the constitutions of Tennessee and the United States. Raulston refused to find an act of the state legislature unconstitutional. With its opening argument defeated, the defense shifted its strategy. An ACLU lawyer, Arthur Garfield Hays, held that the prosecution not only had to prove that Scopes had taught evolution but also that at the same time he had denied the biblical account. Darrow hoped to convince the jury that the Bible contained differing creation accounts. He intended to show that while Scopes may have taught what was contrary to Fundamentalism, he had not violated the beliefs of millions of other Christians. This approach depended on the judge permitting the introduction as evidence of scientific testimony by teams of scholars.

On Friday morning, the seventeenth, Judge Raulston upheld a motion by the state to exclude all scientific testimony from the trial. The defense was devastated. It was rendered incapable of entering evidence concerning the meaning of evolution or interpretations of the Bible. The ruling also hindered the future opportunities for the defense to appeal in higher courts, since evidence would be lacking in the records of the district court. Darrow was furious. He attacked Raulston with scorching sarcasm. The judge in turn found Darrow in contempt of court.

The following Monday morning the trial was convened on the courthouse lawn. Inside, the sweltering heat had become unbearable, and there were mounting fears that the floor would collapse under the weight of so many people. Hays wrapped up some remaining legal technicalities and then sprung the defense's last-ditch effort that Darrow had planned the night before. The defense called Bryan to the stand. The lead prosecution lawyer objected, but Judge Raulston overruled the objection. Bryan was sixty-five years old, in failing health, and had not been in a courtroom for twenty-eight years. He had previously stated that Christians should not let atheists pose questions and force Christians to answer them. Nevertheless, Bryan permitted himself to be questioned as an expert witness on the literal interpretation of the Bible. Outwardly confident, Bryan moved to take the stand. This was the moment the Fundamentalists had been waiting for.

The questioning began with Darrow slowly and consistently prodding, trying to force Bryan to admit that the Bible could not always be taken literally. The interrogation dragged on for an hour and a half. Finally, Bryan, flustered, complained that "the purpose [of this examination] is to cast ridicule on everybody who believes in the Bible, and I am perfectly willing that the world shall know that these gentlemen have no other purpose than ridiculing every Christian who believes in the Bible."

Darrow retorted, "We have the purpose of preventing bigots and ignoramuses from controlling the education of the United States, and you know it and that is all.''

Darrow continued his attack on minute scriptural points, pushing Bryan's claim that everything in the Bible was literally true. Even the crowd, which was largely illiterate, began to notice that Bryan was not entirely consistent. Again and again, Darrow forced Bryan to admit that he could not reconcile apparent conflicts and that he had never thought about many of the issues that Darrow raised. In the end, Bryan disappointed even the staunchest of his Fundamentalist following. He wavered on the crucial question of whether the days mentioned in Genesis were twenty-four-hour periods. Under Darrow's questioning, Bryan admitted that they might have been longer periods, covering millions of years.

Monday was drawing to a close as Darrow brought Bryan to bay.

DARROW: [After an exchange about Adam and Eve and the apple] Do you think that is why the serpent is compelled to crawl upon his belly?

BRYAN: I believe that.

DARROW: Have you any idea how the snake went before that time?

BRYAN: No, sir.

DARROW: Do you know whether he walked on his tail or not?

BRYAN: No, sir, I have no way to know.
(Laughter in the courtroom)

DARROW: Now, you refer to the cloud that was put in the heaven after the flood as the rainbow. Do you believe in that?

BRYAN: Read it.

DARROW: All right, Mr. Bryan, I will read it for you.

BRYAN: Your Honor, I think I can shorten this testimony. The only purpose Mr. Darrow has is to slur at the Bible, but I will answer his question. I will answer it all at once, and I have no objection in the world. I want the world to know that this man who does not believe in God is trying to use a court in Tennessee—

DARROW: I object to that.

BRYAN: —to slur at it, and while it will require time, I am willing to take it.

DARROW: I object to your statement. I am examining you on your fool ideas that no intelligent Christian on earth believes.

THE COURT: Court is adjourned until 9:00 tomorrow morning.

When court resumed the next day, Tuesday the twenty-first, Judge Raulston ruled the previous day's questioning of Bryan inadmissible as evidence. Darrow relinquished the defense, hoping to find grounds for an appeal. As a matter of expediency, Judge Raulston charged the jury to find Scopes guilty. The jury returned their verdict in nine minutes. John

Scopes was called to the bench and pronounced guilty. As he turned to the crowd, his glance fell on Bryan, an exhausted and broken man. People rushed past Bryan to shake Darrow's hand.

Scopes moved to the fringe of the crowd and slumped into an empty chair at the defense table. Questions tumbled through his mind. What had really taken place during the past week? Had he been on trial, or had it been William Jennings Bryan who was the defendant? Had agnosticism prevailed over Christianity? Were science and the Christian faith actually incompatible?

SELECTED BIBLIOGRAPHY

Aymar, Brandt and Sagarin, Edward. *Laws and Trials That Created History*. New York: Crown Publishers, 1974.

Ginger, Ray. *Six Days or Forever*. Chicago: Quadrangle Books, 1969.

Grebstein, Sheldon N. *Monkey Trial*. Boston: Houghton Mifflin, 1960.

Levine, Lawrence. *Defender of the Faith*. New York: Oxford University Press, 1965.

Marsden, George M. *Fundamentalism and American Culture: The Shaping of Twentieth-Century Evangelicalism, 1870-1925*. New York: Oxford University Press, 1980.

Russell, C. Allyn. *Voices of American Fundamentalism*. Philadelphia: Westminster Press, 1976.

Reinhold Niebuhr and World War

This case was prepared by Ronald C. White, Jr.

Reinhold Niebuhr read with furrowed brow the newspaper account of Prime Minister Neville Chamberlain's meeting with Chancellor Adolph Hitler in Munich in September 1938. The immediate issue was the fate of a portion of Czechoslovakia called the Sudentenland, but Niebuhr knew the larger issue was peace or war in Europe. What role America should assume in the growing tensions in Europe was the subject of heated public and personal debate. Niebuhr, a professor at Union Theological Seminary in New York, was a leading participant in these debates. No ivory-tower theologian, his voice was heard in both religious and political quarters. For ten years he had been making up his mind about the momentous issues of war and peace in the public arena of lectures, articles, and books. Attracted to pacifism in the aftermath of World War I, Niebuhr struggled in the 1930s to expound a "Christian realism," which caused him to question pacifism on both political and theological grounds.

Niebuhr knew this was no time to step away from controversy even though he had received dire warnings from his doctors. Both attacked and applauded, Niebuhr was approaching a state of physical collapse. In the United States apprehension at the growing power of Nazism was balanced by the desire to stay out of the quarrels in old Europe. Many in this country viewed Chamberlain's mission with hope, but Niebuhr was deeply alarmed. What should he say and do?

EARLY LIFE

Reinhold Niebuhr was born in Wright City, Missouri, on the first day of summer in 1892. The children of Lydia and Gustav Niebuhr enjoyed a rich family life together. Their father was a pastor of the Evangelical Synod, an offshoot of the Prussian Church Synod that contained both

149

Lutheran and Reformed elements. In 1902, shortly after the father had accepted a call to a parish in Lincoln, Illinois, he asked his ten-year-old son,

> "Have you thought, Reinhold, about what you want to be?"
> "Yes."
> "What?"
> "A minister."
> "Why?"
> "Because you are the most interesting man in town."

Preparation for ministry meant education. Reinhold graduated from Elmhurst College, a small denominational school in Illinois, in 1910, and from Eden Theological Seminary in St. Louis in 1913. A larger world was opened to him when he spent two years of study at Yale Divinity School.

PARISH

In the tradition of the Evangelical Synod, all of his education was to prepare Niebuhr to be a pastor. At the age of twenty-three he accepted a call to the Bethel Evangelical Church in Detroit. Here he would serve until 1928. During these thirteen years the congregation grew tenfold, from 65 to 656 members.

Niebuhr was an able preacher and pastor to his congregation, but his ministry could never be contained by the walls of a church building. His prophetic understanding of social justice was shaped by his proximity to the Ford Motor Company, where he encountered the disjuncture between the myth of Henry Ford as benefactor and the reality of the conditions the people who worked in his factories had to put up with.

Niebuhr embarked upon the pastorate just as Europe was being plunged into war. In those years the young Niebuhr was an enthusiastic support-er of President Woodrow Wilson. When Wilson led the United States into war in 1917, Niebuhr supported this crusade "to make the world safe for democracy."

But the conference in Versailles to end the war and inaugurate peace shook Niebuhr's idealism. "Gradually the whole horrible truth about the war is being revealed," he said. "Every new book destroys some further illusion. How can we ever again believe anything when we compare the solemn pretensions of statesmen with the cynically conceived secret treaties?''

How could Niebuhr reconcile the reality of Versailles with the idealism of Wilson? Here was the beginning of Niebuhr's lifelong wrestling with the perils of "Christian idealism." He came to regard Wilson as "the typical product of the manse who trusted too much in the power of words.''

PACIFISM

In 1923 Niebuhr was invited to visit the Ruhr, a portion of Germany now under French occupation through a provision of the Versailles Treaty. This experience of the peace of Versailles left a vivid impression. He encountered German animosity to what was often brutal French behavior. "The Ruhr cities are the closest thing to hell I have ever seen. I never knew that you could see hatred with the naked eye.''

These weeks in the Ruhr confirmed Niebuhr's embrace of pacifism. Typical of his sentiments in the 1920s were words he penned in 1927: "I think I see clearly that civilizations are not successfully protected by force and that armaments aggravate fears and fears hatreds. I am therefore a pacifist.''

Niebuhr joined with many of his contemporaries in a declaration for peace and against war. To help translate words into action, he became national chairman of the Fellowship of Reconciliation (FOR), a leading organization advocating an active pacifism. For Niebuhr this pacifism was rooted in the bold affirmation that Christians must choose between the claims of the gospel and the values of the world. Writing in 1929 in *Leaves from the Notebook of a Tamed Cynic,* he said, "I am done with this war business. I hope I can make that resolution stick.''

As Niebuhr's friend and colleague John Bennett has pointed out, Niebuhr was never an absolute pacifist. His relentless honesty drove him always to look at issues from all sides. Thus in the article in which he declares himself to be a pacifist he also wonders out loud about his moorings. "Would I be as good a pacifist if I belonged to an unsatisfied nation rather than to a satisfied one?'' Three years later he affirmed that the "judgments of the church on war and peace represent a clear gain over previous generations," but in the same article he muses that "only the day of crisis will reveal . . . whether our present convictions on war

and peace are the result of nausea or of a genuine understanding of the
moral issues involved in international strife."

CRITIQUE OF PACIFISM,

The day of crisis was fast approaching. The course of events both in
America and in Europe and Niebuhr's continuing theological pilgrimage
combined to challenge and then to change the advocate of pacifism.

His first substantial critique of pacifism appeared in *Moral Man and
Immoral Society,* published in 1932. This significant volume signaled a
break with both liberal theology and pacifism. Here Niebuhr presents the
idea that there is no intrinsic difference between violent and nonviolent
resistance. Both can restrain liberty and both can destroy life and property. But if he opened a door to violence in this book, Niebuhr also sought
to place limits on the sorts of violence he would consider morally per-
missible. "If violence can be justified at all, its terror must have the
tempo of a surgeon's skill and healing must follow quickly upon its
wounds." Stemming from a Marxist bias that he would later critique, the
burden of his remarks about violence here were in relation to the quest for
justice in the class struggle in the United States.

The context of this struggle involved Niebuhr's leadership in the FOR.
Religious idealists in the Fellowship were opposing strikes organized by
labor unions on the grounds that such activities violated the law of love.
Niebuhr opposed this point of view as politically irrelevant. On theological grounds, he argued, this meant that pacifists were preferring
injustice if the path to a higher justice involved resistance. On the domestic scene Niebuhr first became persuaded that coercion and resistance
were necessary in the social struggle for justice.

It was ten years after Niebuhr's trip to the Ruhr that Adolph Hitler
came to power in Germany. Already in 1931 Niebuhr had expressed
alarm at the peril to peace posed by German animosity over Versailles
and the ominous sounds coming from "the Hitler movement." In 1934,
five years before Hitler would invade Poland, Niebuhr read the signs of
the times. "It is difficult . . . to see how Hitler's Germany can finally
avoid war with either France or Poland." In 1936 Niebuhr supported
League of Nations sanctions against Italy because of its invasion of
Ethiopia. He wrote at that time, "unwillingness to run some risk of war
in the present moment means certain war in the future."

Niebuhr's critique of pacifism developed in the late thirties as he saw
the world threatened by Nazi tyranny. Increasingly he believed that the

pacifists were making it difficult to resist that tyranny. Some pacifists were acting in common cause with isolationists to keep America out of war. In this country there was the "America First" movement, while in Britain there were the pro-Munich conservatives.

The rejection of pacifism was based on both political and theological grounds. For many Americans, Gandhi became the model of the way of love. But Niebuhr thought it foolish to compare British imperialism with Nazi tyranny. Gandhi's nonviolent campaign had a chance of success because he could appeal to the moral conscience of the British. In the crisis the world was then facing, Niebuhr rejected this kind of pacifism as politically irrelevant.

Niebuhr always distinguished between two kinds of religious pacifism. He was appreciative of certain Mennonite groups that espoused an ethic of agape without proposing their pacifism as a strategy for political solutions. They simply disavowed political goals and sought to live out the kingdom ideal individually and in small communities.

But most American religious pacifism was of a different kind. Niebuhr believed that its well-intentioned proponents distorted the New Testament message. It was his belief that they changed the ethic of nonresistance taught in the Sermon on the Mount into an ethic of nonviolent resistance. Espousing a "politics of the cross," they preached religious absolutes at every turn.

Ultimately Niebuhr's rejection of pacifism was theological. He accused the leading pacifists of failing to do justice to the Reformation doctrines of human nature and justification by faith and charged that they substituted in their place a sectarian perfectionism that placed human beings above the sins of the world. In a letter to a pacifist Niebuhr said, "Your difficulty is that you want to try to live in history without sinning." Pacifism and liberalism, for Niebuhr, both foundered on the doctrine of sin, both failed to see the limits inherent in human nature.

Niebuhr believed that the doctrine of justification by faith was profoundly relevant in the present crisis because it secures our ground in the midst of moral ambiguities. To live as justifed by grace through faith is to take with the utmost seriousness the tensions and conflicts all around us but to be grounded in God's ultimate victory. One of Niebuhr's favorite New Testament texts was 2 Corinthians 4:8, in which Paul speaks of being "perplexed, but not driven to despair."

Even when "realism" demanded this strong critique, Niebuhr was still able to appreciate the witness of pacifism. Just a year before Munich, Niebuhr observed that "the church would be the poorer and its counsels in greater danger of corruption by popular hysteria if it lacked the pacifist testimony." Why was it so important to hear this testimony? Niebuhr answered that "war is such a terrible catastrophe in modern life that anyone who participates in it ought to do so only with a very uneasy conscience." Our consciences will "be kept uneasy by those who find it impossible to reconcile war with Christ."

CONTROVERSY

Niebuhr was perplexed in September 1938. The London *Times* hailed the deliberations at Munich as a triumph of reason over force. "At the moment when the current racing toward the precipice seemed irresistible, it was the leadership of the British Prime Minister that showed how immense were the forces ranged on the side of reason against violence." Many American newspapers echoed these sentiments.

As Niebuhr raised his voice, he became more and more enmeshed in controversy, more and more the target of attack. His own pilgrimage was written out in a series of articles printed in *The Christian Century,* but now the pages of this leading liberal religious periodical were given over to an advocacy of pacifism and not infrequently a criticism of Niebuhr.

As Europe teetered on the brink, it might seem that Niebuhr had come to espouse a position similar to that of those who had supported the Great War. But there was a critical difference. That World War was embraced as a crusade. Niebuhr had joined a disillusioned generation when it was discovered that the crusaders had blood on their hands. Now he warned against the "self-righteousness" of the allied nations. He was opposed to National Socialism, but that did not stop him from insisting that our own national policies also have be held up to moral judgment.

Casting aside his doctor's warnings, Niebuhr decided that the events surrounding Munich demanded words, not silence. Always one to see the humor in the stress of controversy, Niebuhr confided to a friend, "I do wish that they'd hate Hitler more and me less."

Now that the Munich settlement had been made, Niebuhr took his pen in hand. "We can't really understand in what sense the peace of Munich is to be celebrated because at least it postponed the war. . . . Is it really true that to postpone a war is to add to the chance of its ultimate avoidance?"

Niebuhr considered what his own course should be. He was aware that some of his friends felt he should tone down his questioning and critique. Well-intentioned people urged him to give peace a chance. But was this really peace, or was it appeasement that could only lead to war? He sensed that the time was rapidly approaching when America would no longer be able to enjoy the luxury of being a spectator separated from the conflict by the Atlantic. At this terrible moment Niebuhr agonized over what he should say to the churches and the nation.

SELECTED BIBLIOGRAPHY

Bingham, June. *Courage to Change: An Introduction to the Life and Thought of Reinhold Niebuhr.* New York: Scribner's, 1961.

Harland, Gordon. *The Thought of Reinhold Niebuhr.* New York: Oxford University Press, 1960.

Meyer, Donald B. *The Protestant Search for Political Realism, 1919-1941.* Berkeley and Los Angeles: University of California Press, 1960.

Kegley, Charles W. and Bretall, Robert W., eds. *Reinhold Niebuhr: His Religious, Social, and Political Thought.* New York: Macmillan, 1956.

Niebuhr, Reinhold. *Christianity and Power Politics.* New York: Scribner's, 1940.

_____. *Leaves from the Notebook of a Tamed Cynic.* Chicago: Willet, Clark & Coldy, 1929.

_____. *Moral Man and Immoral Society: A Study of Ethics and Politics.* New York: Scribner's, 1932.

Stone, Ronald H. *Reinhold Niebuhr: Prophet to Politicians.* Nashville: Abingdon Press, 1971.

NOTE: A good way to grasp the evolution of Reinhold Niebuhr's thinking in the 1930s is to read his articles in *The Christian Century.*

John Courtney Murray, the American Experience, and Religious Freedom at Vatican II

This case was prepared by Roger A. Couture

The meeting about to get under way was one of the most tense that Jesuit priest-theologian John Courtney Murray had ever attended. The Theological Commission now in session was responsible for overseeing all matters pertaining to faith and morals at the Council and so had the authority to decide if and when a particular topic could be discussed and voted on there. The Commission, headed by its strongly traditionalist president, Alfredo Cardinal Ottaviani, had successfully blocked all discussion of religious freedom at the Second Vatican Council thus far by using a simple but effective tactic: since July of 1963—it was now November 11—it had refused to allow printing of the text on religious freedom submitted by the Secretariat for Christian Unity. Unless the Commission now reversed its position and voted to put religious freedom on the Council's agenda, the issue could not be addressed by the Council at its present session—already its second—and its fate beyond that would at best be uncertain.

As he awaited an invitation to speak to the dozen or so cardinals, archbishops, bishops, and other church leaders who made up the Commission, Father Murray was very much aware of another presence in the room: across from him at the end of the table sat his most unrelenting American opponent on church-state issues: Monsignor Joseph C. Fenton of Catholic University in Washington. As soon as the Council had gotten under way in 1962, Fenton had been called to Rome as personal adviser to Cardinal Ottaviani.

THE MAKING OF AN AMERICAN THEOLOGIAN

The path that had led Murray to the Second Vatican Council had been a tortuous one. A native New Yorker, he had first been attracted to the

Society of Jesus in 1920 at the age of sixteen. By the time he began teaching theology at Woodstock College in Woodstock, Maryland, in 1937, he had already spent seven years abroad, three of them in the Philippines teaching Latin and English and four in Rome acquiring a doctorate in theology. But it was life in America—what he would come to call the American experience—that fascinated him the most. He was to try his whole life to articulate its significance for theology and the church.

Murray's intellectual abilities singled him out early to his Jesuit superiors as one capable of serious research and writing. In 1941, just one year after the establishment of *Theological Studies,* Murray was asked to accept the editorship of the quarterly journal that had been designed to provide a sounding-board for the newly emerging American Catholic scholarship. Soon after he also accepted the request that he become religion editor for *America* magazine, a Jesuit-sponsored weekly journal of opinion. Additional recognition came to Murray in 1946 when he was elected to the Board of Directors of the Catholic Theological Society of America (CTSA) at its inaugural meeting in New York. Significantly, at that same meeting two of the theologians elected as officers of the CTSA would soon emerge as determined adversaries of Murray's views: Francis J. Connell, a Redemptorist priest who was elected president, and Joseph Fenton, who was named secretary. Both would be closely associated for years with *The American Ecclesiastical Review,* a journal published in Washington—Fenton would serve as editor from 1944 to 1963—and they would use it as a vehicle for their ongoing campaign against the "new" theology.

Initially, the differences between Connell and Murray had to do with interfaith cooperation and the issues it raised for American Catholics. Already in the early forties Connell had cautioned about ill-advised attempts at rapprochement with other religious groups, stating his fear that the pendulum might already have swung too far with Catholics moving "from bigotry to indifferentism." Other problems Connell anticipated were a "watering down" of the church's teaching on tolerance, on the relationship between church and state, and on the scope of the church's authority.

THE SECULARIST THREAT

Connell's warnings about the danger of indifferentism (often echoed by Fenton) persisted through the years despite Murray's repeated efforts to show that he shared that same general concern but believed that the way to offset the threat was not through isolation. Murray's writings during the 1940s reveal that it was precisely the drift toward secularist humanism that compelled him to advocate greater interfaith understanding and cooperation. Not unrelated to this secularist trend was what Murray perceived and described in the late forties as "the new nativism," a wave of anti-Catholicism that revived many of the features of earlier surges of anti-Catholic feeling in America. One of the principal voices in this movement was Paul Blanshard, who was closely associated with a nondenominational group known as Protestants and Other Americans United for Separation of Church and State (POAU). In his numerous books, Blanshard exhibited a persistent and at times virulent anti-Catholic bias while advocating a secularist-statist philosophy that in Murray's view constituted a much greater threat to the nation than anything Blanshard called attention to in American Catholicism.

As he sought to respond to critics from both within and outside the church in the years after World War II, Murray sensed that it was urgently necessary for the church to articulate clearly its position on religious freedom. It needed to present a position that would be fully compatible with American Catholicism's centuries-long experience within a religiously pluralistic society but that would also allay the fears of those who saw the growth of the church in America as a threat to their own freedom. During the early 1950s Murray attempted to lay the groundwork for such a position.

THE TRADITIONAL VIEW

The starting point of the traditional view (of which Murray became increasingly critical) was its understanding of religious truth and the implications of that truth for life in society. Central to this approach was its claim that only those who accept fully God's one revelation made through Jesus Christ could be said to be in the one truth willed by God. That truth, the traditionalists maintained, is found in its fullness only in the Roman Catholic Church. Thus members of this Church could claim to have a conscience that was not only subjectively upright (sincere) but also in full conformity with the objective truth made known to us through revelation. Since religious freedom is grounded in objective truth, only members of the true church can legitimately claim the right to profess and practice their faith both privately and publicly without interference from the state.

What was the status of those outside the Catholic fold according to such a view? Theirs is a sincere but clearly erroneous conscience. Subjectively it could be presumed that they had made an effort to respond to God's call by adhering to what they judged to be God's revelation; but objectively God's truth, or at least the fullness of it, was not present in them. Thus, since religious freedom can only be rooted in the truth, those outside the church can claim no right to it, or only a very limited right at best. Hence the oft-repeated dictum: "Error has no rights."

As Murray examined the traditionalists' position on religious freedom, he found that it was grounded in an understanding of church and state that went back to the Middle Ages and had subsequently been embodied in some of the Catholic nation-states. In this model, Catholicism was institutionalized as the state religion. Catholics were not only in the majority in such states, but the church enjoyed constitutional recognition and preferential treatment. Historically, this arrangement frequently resulted in the legal repression of all "heresy." The primacy of the spiritual power of the church was affirmed in such a way that the power of the state was included in it and derived from it. Since the prince was responsible for the preservation of the common good and church unity was perceived as essential to political unity, defending the faith against error became a political duty as well as a means of promoting the good of society.

In the traditional view, this kind of close union between church and state—the confessional state or established religion—was acknowledged to be the normal or ideal situation, the "thesis" as it was called, and was considered the only arrangement under which Catholic principles could be applied without reservation. In situations that fell short of this, as in states in which Catholics constituted a minority, a "hypothesis" situation prevailed. There the church would forego its right to legal establishment as the one religion of the state, but it would also resist putting its stamp of approval on the resulting constitutional situation. Such situations were simply tolerated as lesser evils, exceptions to the rule, practical expedients.

AUTHORITY IN THE CHURCH

Fenton and other traditionalists held that this church-state doctrine was the only such formulation that was internally consistent with objective religious truth as found in revelation and as taught consistently and authoritatively by the official Church. As Fenton understood it, the task of the theologian was "only to bring out a clear, certain, and unequivocal expression of the meaning of that message which we know as divine public revelation . . . to present God's own teaching on how the church and state are meant to live together."

As he pursued his research on church and state, it became increasingly clear to Murray that as long as one accepted Fenton's definition of the role of the theologian it would not be possible to challenge effectively the traditional teaching on religious freedom and begin moving in a different direction. What was needed was a shift in method. It was time to abandon the approach based primarily on abstract truth and replace it with a method of interpretation that paid more attention to the historical context in which theological truth developed and was articulated. Murray applied himself to this task anew in the early 1950s, especially in four important articles on the church-state teaching of Pope Leo XIII (1878-1903) published in *Theological Studies* in 1953-54.

Murray's exploration led him to the conclusion that the papal teaching on the relationship of church and state had evolved significantly over the centuries. The model advocating the primacy of the church's spiritual power—still reflected in the church-state theory of the traditionalists—perpetuated a medieval conception drastically revised by later church teaching.

A key contribution of Leo XIII to the church-state doctrine involved the role he assigned to the citizen in society. He recast the basic rationale of church-state interaction in terms of the citizen whom both powers served. The individual who was both church member and citizen became the raison d'être of both institutions. And both church and state were called to a cooperative pattern of life, since both were necessary for the full development of their members.

However, as Murray showed in his 1953-54 articles, Leo XIII did not rise above the political context of nineteenth-century Latin Europe. This meant that he still identified the state with organized human society. As a consequence he still required of the state the kind of total commitment to Christian principles and practice that had been demanded earlier of less differentiated Christian societies. In this perspective he affirmed that the public profession and dissemination of non-Catholic religions could only be tolerated by "Catholic" states.

Tolerance in that sense was still not religious freedom. As the church entered into the twentieth century, religious freedom remained a narrowly conceived and elusive reality. The church would be moved closer to accepting a broader concept under Pius XII, who assumed its leadership just as World War II broke out in Europe in 1939.

RELIGIOUS FREEDOM AND PIUS XII

In the face of totalitarian governments of both right and left and the absolute power claimed by the state, Pius XII attempted to show that citizens are endowed with a complex of rights that protect them against unjust intrusion and allow them to participate in shaping the political system. In a 1945 address, Pius spoke of the person as "the subject, foundation, and end of the social order." The dignity of the human person became a central focus of his thought. As he enumerated "the fundamental rights of the human person" that must be acknowledged and respected in every well-ordered society, Pius affirmed specifically "the right to the private and public worship of God, including action under the impulse of religious charity." The power of governments is limited, he insisted, even as pertains to the repression of error in society.

Despite these significant statements of Pius XII on basic human rights and the concept of limited government, Murray could not find in his writings an explicit affirmation of religious freedom as a human right. What was acknowledged was a civil right within the constitutional framework of democratic society. In addition, Murray could not help but notice that although religious freedom was conceived as broader in application than that, it was almost always advocated primarily for the church. This ambiguity in papal teaching, which persisted even with Pius XII, enabled Murray to continue developing his own thought with a certain amount of freedom. But it also made him vulnerable to accusations of being at variance with official church teaching. With the appearance in 1950 of the encyclical *Humani generis,* which condemned "modern" errors in the church, such accusations were clearly not to be taken lightly.

Humani generis gave Fenton and others in his camp an opportunity to claim support for their position from the highest authority in the church. The position Fenton had argued in countless articles in *The American Ecclesiastical Review* through the 1940s could be summarized as follows: (1) the church's position on church-state relations and religious freedom has been taught with unmistakable clarity by the popes through the centuries and has been definitively articulated in the numerous encyclical letters of Leo XIII; (2) such definitive teaching by the church's highest authority requires all Catholics, including theologians, to give not only external obedience but inner assent as well to the authoritative teaching; and (3) attempts by some theologians to distinguish between the "deposit of genuine Catholic teaching" on the one hand and "notions current at the time the encyclicals were written" that were time-bound and could later be discarded on the other, reflected, Fenton insisted, an attitude "radically destructive of a true Catholic mentality."

As Fenton interpreted it, *Humani generis* discredited once and for all the kind of historical approach he saw exemplified in Murray's work.

NINETEENTH-CENTURY EUROPE AND THE DOCTRINE OF SEPARATION

Prior to Leo XIII, Pius IX in his famous *Syllabus of errors* (1864) had severely criticized the liberal understanding of freedom of conscience, which in his view contradicted the most fundamental duties of all to God and society. In it he condemned as erroneous the proposition that "it is false to say that granting civil liberty to any cult whatsoever and giving to all the full right to openly and publicly discuss and profess any opinions or thoughts they have would more easily corrupt the morals and souls of the people and spread the plague of indifferentism."

According to Fenton, statements such as this invalidated in a decisive way any claim to religious freedom on the part of those who did not belong to the one true church. Murray's response to Fenton was that neither Pius IX nor Leo XIII were in fact condemning the kind of religious freedom that was the unique experience of the various religious groups who found refuge in the United States. What the popes were attacking, he argued, was a European liberal understanding of liberty that was in fact antagonistic to religion.

In contrast, Murray maintained that religious freedom as practiced and guaranteed by law in America was open rather than hostile to religion. As stated in the First Amendment to the Constitution of the United States, the principle of separation of church and state did not embody any bias against religion but rather sought to establish in a religiously pluralistic society a *modus vivendi* in which all religions could develop and thrive without obstacle. Unfortunately, as Murray discovered, the American version of religious freedom was for all practical purposes poorly understood, if it was understood at all, by the nineteenth-century popes, whose vision was limited to a European church and society in deep turmoil.

THE PAPACY AND THE CHURCH IN AMERICA

Despite the enormous distance that separated the church of Rome from the church in America in the nineteenth century, two important papal letters had been sent by Leo XIII to the American bishops at the end of the century. In his ongoing debate with Murray, Fenton repeatedly cited both these letters as decisive proof that Leo had continued to the end to hold the thesis-hypothesis doctrine on church-state questions.

In *Longinqua oceani* (1895), the first papal letter addressed to the young American church, Leo alluded to the division among American bishops concerning the desirability of the no-establishment clause. He then acknowledged that the American system enabled the church to be

> free to live and act without hindrance. Yet, although all this is true, it would be very erroneous to draw the conclusion that in America is to be sought the type of the most desirable status of the Church, or that it would be universally lawful or expedient for State and Church to be, as in America, dissevered and divorced. . . . She [the Church] would bring forth more abundant fruits if, in addition to liberty, she enjoyed the favor of the laws and the patronage of public authority.

Leo XIII's other letter to the American church came in 1899 and was entitled *Testem benevolentiae*. It warned of certain errors "called by some Americanism." It did not deal specifically with the church-state issue but rather with an approach to official church teaching that, if it were indeed followed, could constitute a watering down or even a rejection of that teaching. *Testem* described this approach as follows: "in order the more easily to bring over to Catholic doctrine those who dissent from it, the Church ought to adapt herself somewhat to our advanced civilization, and, relaxing her ancient rigor, show some indulgence to modern theories and methods." Fenton insisted in 1949 that this letter of Leo XIII met the requirements of a "real definition" of doctrine by the magisterium. Thus the only appropriate response on the part of Catholics was to accept the traditional teaching on church-state relationships as found in Leo XIII's many pronouncements and repeated faithfully by the popes after him.

The publication of Pius XII's *Humani generis* in 1950 had been viewed as a triumph and vindication by Fenton. So too, three years later, was an important speech given in Rome by Cardinal Ottaviani, an influential adviser to the pope and head of the Holy Office, the Roman curia or agency responsible for all matters of doctrine in the church.

CARDINAL OTTAVIANI ON CHURCH AND STATE

On 2 March 1953, Cardinal Ottaviani gave an address at the Lateran University in Rome entitled "Church and State: Some Present Problems in the Light of Teachings of Pope Pius XII.'' Because of the prestige of his position in the Vatican, what he had to say about the church-state issue could not help but take on special significance for all involved in the ongoing controversy. In substance Ottaviani made two major points, both contradicting Murray's position as he was in the process of elaborating it in his 1953-54 *Theological'Studies* articles on Leo XIII. Ottaviani affirmed (1) that only the "confessional state" or established religion meets Leo XIII's strict requirements as outlined in his many official teachings and (2) that the position of Leo XIII was still taught by the popes who had followed him, including the reigning pontiff, Pius XII. Recognizing in Cardinal Ottaviani a powerful ally for the traditionalists, Fenton immediately published a translation of Ottaviani's discourse in *The American Ecclesiastical Review.*

As for Murray, he found it difficult to assess accurately the significance of Cardinal Ottaviani's address, especially how much support he had from Pius XII. A month later, in April, Murray suffered a severe setback; he was hospitalized for "extreme fatigue, rooted in a cardiac insufficiency" and ordered to take an indefinite period of rest.

While recovering, Murray received a letter from Rome that provided some encouragement. A Jesuit who was private secretary to Pius XII, Robert Leiber, wrote to him in June assuring him that Ottaviani's March discourse reflected only the Cardinal's private view and that it had no "official or semi-official" authority. Since Ottaviani had referred specifically to Murray's approach as one of those at variance with papal teaching, Leiber encouraged Murray to clarify his position, at least by writing a personal letter to the cardinal. A month later Murray was still not fully reassured: "The discourse by Cardinal Ottaviani in the spring," he wrote in July to a friend, "may possibly precipitate something in Rome."

In November a letter from the American representative at the Jesuit headquarters in Rome confirmed that Murray's fears were not without foundation. The letter, addressed to Murray's provincial superior in New York, stated enigmatically: "I think the time has come for Fr. Murray to put in simple, clear statements his full, present position regarding the church-state question and to send it to me for Fr. General." Murray's still feeble condition did not enable him to provide the requested statements immediately, but he did seek some clarification of the intent of the request: "It would help," he stated warily, "to know whether I am speaking into a Roman climate of hostility or receptivity."

Unexpected reassurance came in early December from none other than Pius XII. Even before seeing the full text of his address given on 6 December 1953 (entitled *Ci riesce*), Murray described it to a friend, on the basis of newspaper accounts, as "clearly the pope's own reply to the famous discourse of Cardinal Ottaviani. And it is an important disavowal of the position taken by the latter."

Though in the months that followed *Ci riesce,* Fenton claimed in writing that the allocution by Pius XII in no way contradicted Ottaviani's earlier speech, Murray's optimism continued growing to the point that he decided to defend his own interpretation publicly. On 25 March 1954 Murray delivered a forceful lecture on *Ci riesce* at the Catholic University in Washington. The reactions soon revealed that he had underestimated the strength and influence of his adversaries.

MURRAY SILENCED

Murray learned a short while later that Cardinal Ottaviani had sent a letter on the first of April to Cardinal Spellman of New York stating that he had been offended by Murray's lecture and seriously questioned the accuracy of his interpretation of papal statements. A year later, in July 1955, Murray was informed that Jesuit censors in Rome to whom he had sent a final article on Leo XIII had recommended that the piece not be published. "Fr. General," he was told, "agrees with the verdict."

A discouraged Murray responded by thanking his informant for "his delicate way of saying, You're through!" The return letter from Rome tried to alleviate the pain of the blow Murray had received, but it left no doubt that he was being silenced on the church-state issue: "You are far from through, I hope," the letter stated; "but let the State-Church question rest for the present." The "present," as it turned out, would extend over several years.

Three years later, on 8 October 1958, news arrived that Pius XII had died. While it would take some time before there would be a general recognition of the change in mood that John XXIII's pontificate would bring, the pope's announcement in January 1959 that he would soon call an "Ecumenical Council for the Universal Church" caught the world by surprise and gave rise to hopes for a renewed and more open Catholic church on the part of many, both within and outside the church.

By 1960 Murray felt confident enough to publish one of his major works, *We Hold These Truths: Catholic Reflections on the American Proposition.* Addressing a wide range of social and political issues, the book also touched on the church-state question and religious freedom in several of its chapters. It attracted considerable attention. Appearing shortly before the 1960 election of President Kennedy, it was considered by some to have had a not insignificant impact in some quarters on the outcome of that election.

Not everyone responded positively, however, to Murray's book. In his review for *The American Ecclesiastical Review,* Fenton assailed Murray's position, calling it into question on doctrinal grounds and characterizing it as an example of the "carelessness" and "sympathy for the liberalism of the day" that he saw as undermining the church's official teaching. Thus as the date for the opening of the Second Vatican Council approached—it was slated to begin in October 1962—the opposition to Murray's views on the church-state question continued unabated. Two events in the first year of the Council revealed how serious and influential this opposition really was.

PERSISTENT OPPOSITION

First, as the Council got under way in the fall of 1962, Murray was not invited to take part in the First Session as a *peritus* (expert). Worse still, he soon learned that because of certain interventions apparently channeled through the Apostolic Delegate in Washington, he was in fact "disinvited" from having any part in conciliar deliberations.

The other disturbing development for Murray occurred in the spring of 1963. Again through the intervention of the Apostolic Delegate in Washington, Murray and three other prominent theologians (Godfrey Diekmann, Gustave Weigel, and Hans Küng) were specifically banned from giving lectures at the Catholic University. Reactionary elements were clearly gaining the upper hand once again in sectors of the American church. However, events in the months that followed brought the first indications that the traditionalist forces at the Council in Rome might no longer be in full control. On 4 April 1963 Murray was informed that he was being called to Rome as a theological adviser. The invitation, he learned, came as a result of pressure exerted by none other than Cardinal Spellman of New York, who had not been known until then for having much sympathy for liberal theologians.

Then, a week after Murray received his letter of invitation to the Council, John XXIII published his landmark encyclical *Pacem in terris,* wherein he proclaimed the "dignity of the human person" as the very foundation of a wide range of human rights. Specifically included among these rights was the right "to honor God according to the sincere dictates of one's own conscience, and therefore the right to practice one's religion privately and publicly."

Despite this authoritative statement, Murray would discover as he arrived in Rome that much remained to be done before a significant statement on religious freedom could emerge from the Council.

PREPARING A DRAFT ON RELIGIOUS FREEDOM

Initially a subcommission of the Secretariat for Christian Unity, the Roman agency responsible for ecumenical affairs worldwide, had prepared a draft statement on religious freedom. In the months preceding the First Session, which began in October 1962, Archbishop Shehan of Baltimore had sent the Secretariat's first two drafts to Murray for his reactions. Murray had expressed serious disappointment with these texts and characterized them as an attempt to avoid the central issue by simply stating everyone's right to religious freedom without elaborating the theoretical rationale for such a right. If that were all the Council did, Murray warned, the traditionalists would have triumphed once again, since such "practical" statements would look "like sheer concessions to 'today's circumstances'"; in other words, they would leave the traditional position in place unchallenged. "We have a heaven-sent opportunity to effect a genuine development of doctrine in this matter," Murray went on to say. "The opportunity should not be missed."

In Rome the Secretariat for Christian Unity, which had produced the first drafts, found itself in a constant struggle for jurisdiction with the powerful Theological Commission headed by Cardinal Ottaviani. Originally, the statement on religious freedom was to be incorporated into the schema on the "Church." This meant that it touched on matters of doctrine, and so the Theological Commission judged it to be outside the scope of the Secretariat and primarily its own responsibility. On that basis, the Theological Commission had submitted its own separate draft on religious freedom to the Central Commission of the Council—a draft in which it decisively reaffirmed the traditional teaching. Subsequent negotiations between the Secretariat and the Theological Commission had finally broken down completely in August 1962, with the result that the issue of religious freedom never reached the Council floor for discussion during its first session in the fall of 1962.

Shortly after the opening of that first session, however, Pope John XXIII had moved to resolve the stalemate. He elevated the Secretariat for Christian Unity, a permanent office of the Vatican, to an equal rank with the ad hoc commissions set up specifically for the Council, one of which was the Theological Commission. Its revised status authorized the Secretariat to present its own schemas to the Council. After the end of the first session, the Secretariat had produced a new draft—shorter than the previous ones and more in line with its more progressive approach to religious freedom than the text proposed by the Theological Commission. The new draft of the Secretariat was finally approved 30 May 1963 after further revisions. A later session of the Secretariat then voted to incorporate the text on religious freedom into the schema on ecumenism rather than that on the church. All that remained was to submit the text to Cardinal Cicognani of the Central Commission for printing, which the Secretariat did in July, well in advance of the second session scheduled to start in October.

However, despite the pope's reinforcing of the Secretariat's position within the Council and the fact that the text on religious freedom was now to be part of the schema on ecumenism, an area for which the Secretariat for Christian Unity had special competence, the Theological Commission under Ottaviani continued to oppose adamantly any conciliar discussion of religious freedom by holding up the printing of the Secretariat's proposed text. When Murray arrived in Rome for the second session, the topic of religious freedom still was not on the agenda of the Council.

Murray also discovered that the Secretariat's revised text, while an improvement on earlier versions, still contained what he considered to be severe limitations. For one thing, he felt that the arguments presented in support of religious freedom did not go far enough. One of the arguments based religious freedom on the right to follow one's conscience, even if in error; the other based it on the freedom of the act of faith as response to God. Another deficiency in the text, as Murray saw it, was the fact that it placed limits on religious freedom in terms of the state's duty to protect and promote the *common* good rather than the *public* good, which Murray understood in a narrower and more precise sense less open to abuse by the state.

MEETING WITH THE THEOLOGICAL COMMISSION

Despite his reservations about the proposed text, Murray knew, as did the Secretariat and others who were anxious to see religious freedom openly discussed at the Council, that it would never happen unless the Theological Commission's stranglehold was broken. By early November, a month into the second session, it had become clear that Ottaviani would not budge, that he would in fact do all within his power to stop the issue of religious freedom from being discussed on the Council floor. He was even rumored to have gone to Pope Paul VI in order to convince him that the issue of religious freedom should be tabled. However, as the months passed, many of the bishops in Rome were beginning to show impatience with the delays. Notable among these were the American bishops. As the stalemate continued, a majority of them signed a petition presented to the pope in their name by Cardinal Spellman urging that the text on religious freedom be discussed at the second meeting.

A few days later, Father Murray was informed that a meeting of the Theological Commission had been called for the eleventh of November with instructions from the pope that a vote was to be taken regarding the submission of the Secretariat's draft to the Council. Murray and a few other theological advisers were being invited to attend the meeting, at which representatives of the Secretariat for Christian Unity would also be present.

As the 11 November meeting got under way, Murray was very conscious of the fact that Cardinal Ottaviani had thus far been able to keep a majority of the Commission members on his side. If whoever spoke at the meeting—and Murray had been told that he and other theological advisers would likely be invited to address the group—did not succeed in changing the minds of at least some of the bishops on the Commission, all the efforts made thus far to prepare the way for an open and forward-looking discussion of the issue of religious freedom at the Council would come to naught. As he reflected on what he would say when called on, Murray could not but sense the significance of the moment. Little could he have anticipated, even a few months before, that this moment would bring him face to face with the two churchmen who had been his most powerful and unrelenting adversaries on religious freedom: Cardinal Ottaviani and Monsignor Fenton.

SELECTED BIBLIOGRAPHY

Anderson, Floyd, ed. *Council Daybook: Vatican II, Sessions 1 and 2*. Washington: National Catholic Welfare Conference, 1965.

Murray, John Courtney. *The Problem of Religious Freedom*. Westminster, Md.: Newman Press, 1965.

————. *We Hold These Truths: Catholic Reflections on the American Proposition*.

Pelotte, Donald E. *John Courtney Murray: Theologian in Conflict.* New York: Paulist Press, 1975.

Regan, Richard J. *Conflict and Consensus: Religious Freedom and the Second Vatican Council.* New York: Macmillan, 1967.

Vatican Council II. *Declaration on Religious Freedom,* in *The Documents of Vatican II,* ed. Walter M. Abbott. New York: America Press, 1966.

Martin Luther King: Justice, Peace, and Civil Rights

This case was prepared by Louis B. Weeks

The dilemma confronting Martin Luther King, Jr., in the summer of 1965 threatened the civil rights movement of which he was the acknowledged leader. On the sixth of August, King had stood in front of a statue of Abraham Lincoln in the rotunda of the Capitol as President Lyndon Baines Johnson signed the voting rights bill. After a decade of struggle and tragedy, this legislation signaled a triumph, and much of the credit for it was being given to King. But in these same days he was becoming convinced that he could no longer remain silent about the nation's involvement in Vietnam. He told his closest aides in the Southern Christian Leadership Conference (SCLC), "I'm not going to sit by and see the war escalate without saying something about it." He was becoming convinced that civil rights and Vietnam were not issues that could be neatly separated. "It is worthless to talk about integrating if there is no world to integrate in The war in Vietnam must be stopped."

King's staff and followers were deeply divided over the linking of civil rights in America to peace in southeast Asia. Roy Wilkins, Whitney Young, and other civil rights leaders urged King to avoid criticism of United States foreign policy and to concentrate on consolidation of gains for America's black population. Financial advisors warned that the SCLC would lose many donors if King spoke out. Even pacifist Bayard Rustin cautioned King against endangering his carefully nurtured relationship with President Johnson. On the other hand, antiwar leaders pointed to the disproportionate involvement of America's poor blacks in the casualty figures among the armed forces, to the relationship of nonviolent civil rights activity with pacifism on a global scale, and to the fabric in which matters of conscience were integrally woven.

Since his Montgomery days, King had often denounced the "madness of militarism" in his speeches. Earlier in 1965 in Los Angeles he had declared that matters of domestic justice and foreign affairs were "inextricably bound." He had quipped that "it's nice to drink milk at an unsegregated lunch counter—but not when there's strontium 90 in it." By the same token, he had sometimes avoided the broader issues, as when he restricted himself to speaking only on civil rights and free speech at a rally in behalf of the unseated Georgia representative Julian Bond, for example. He could not continue to enjoy the luxury of indecision. As an international figure, a moral leader, and a Christian minister, he would certainly be forced to decide.

BACKGROUND

Ever since the beginning of black immigration to America, questions of justice and peace were bound inseparably with religious matters. Almost all importation of slaves had occurred in an atmosphere of violence and severe oppression. During colonial times, theologians had sometimes even debated the very humanity of Africans. Did human rights and Christian evangelism pertain to slaves? Generally American Christians had considered slavery an expedient but immoral institution. Gradually, however, different responses to the issues had divided Americans of European origin. Some had argued that slavery served to "Christianize" blacks and "fit" them for eventual participation in all society. Others had sought an end to slavery and the return of Afro-Americans to their "homelands." Still others perceived slavery an institution with which Christians should not interfere. A fourth view emerged that black Americans should enjoy the full benefits of free membership in the society they helped to construct.

Meanwhile, free black leaders, slave preachers, and white evangelists did work to bring the gospel to a vast majority of American black people. In Christianity, slave owners saw a means of keeping their chattel obedient. Thousands of sermons focused on Ephesians 6 or Colossians 3: "Slaves, be obedient. . . ." Black Americans learned the Judeo-Christian traditions of Exodus, freedom, and human dignity from the Bible stories and hymns. Their own hymns offered the promise of liberation and the impingement of God's kingdom on everyday life.

After the Civil War, with the explicit enfranchisement that the U.S. Constitution guaranteed in the thirteenth, fourteenth, and fifteenth amendments, black Americans began the arduous process of claiming their rights and exercising their responsibilities. White racism reasserted itself thoroughly in a bevy of "Jim Crow" laws that permitted racial segregation. Black churches, growing as separate institutions, provided solace, hope, and a limited sphere of independent life for members. Some few blacks also participated in predominantly white denominations.

Black preaching gave leadership to these churches and gave voice to wider aspirations as well. When whites committed reprehensible acts of violence against blacks—the lynching of hundreds during the early twentieth century, for example—black ministers frequently made appeals to law and human rights on behalf of their flocks. When blacks were called upon to do menial chores in the American efforts in World War I, black preachers such as Francis J. Grimke had called upon America to give human rights to all citizens, including minorities.

Following World War II, as the American black population began to agitate for full civil rights, other black professionals were extremely important. Black insurance company owners, professors, teachers, undertakers, and entrepreneurs gave a financial and articulate base for the movement. Black lawyers had been constructing the legal base for decades from which court cases sprang. And whites frequently served in cooperative endeavors. But it was natural that a black preacher emerged from the black churches to lead the struggle.

MARTIN LUTHER KING, JR.

Martin Luther King, Jr., was born in 1929, in the family of Martin Luther and Alberta Williams King. His father, minister of the Ebenezer Baptist Church, had led that congregation in combating racism while proclaiming the gospel in Atlanta, Georgia. Young "Mike" King grew up amid racial segregation, relatively secure in a loving family of moderate circumstance. He experienced the humiliation of white racism on occasion—a friendship with a white playmate forbidden by that boy's parents, a surprise slap in the face from a white woman in a department store—but he grew up generally insulated in Atlanta's sizable black community, in the Booker T. Washington public high school, and in the stimulating intellectual climate of Morehouse College, which he entered at age fifteen.

Called to become a minister, he went North to enter Crozer Seminary of the American Baptist Convention, where he excelled in theological disciplines. Subsequently, he studied at Boston University, graduating with a Ph.D. in systematic theology in 1955. At Boston, he met Coretta

Scott, a graduate student in music at the New England Conservatory. They married in 1953, and in 1954 they moved to Montgomery, Alabama, where King became pastor of the Dexter Avenue Baptist Church.

Rosa Parks, arrested in December 1955 for refusing to relinquish to a white man her seat on a bus, touched off the protest against segregation in Montgomery that propelled King into leadership of the civil rights movement. He became president first of the Montgomery Improvement Association and then of the Southern Christian Leadership Conference, which he helped to organize. In 1960 he moved back to Atlanta and began service as copastor with his father of the Ebenezer Baptist Church. International recognition of King's leadership came after his organization of the 1963 March on Washington and his address on that occasion from the steps of the Lincoln Memorial.

"Five score years ago, a great American in whose symbolic shadow we stand, signed the Emancipation Proclamation," King began. He proceeded to recount the sad history of oppression, a preacher's sermon for society in general and the gathered 250,000 in particular. "America has defaulted on its promissory note," he declared. Nevertheless, he encouraged black people not to drink "from the cup of bitterness or hatred" but to strive for civil rights. Abandoning his prepared text, King told the audience, "I have a dream today!" He drew upon the words of the patriotic song "My Country, 'tis of Thee," upon the phrases of the Declaration of Independence, upon the biblical images of the coming Day of the Lord, and upon his own experience of American aspirations.

> When we let freedom ring, when we let it ring from every village and every hamlet, from every state and every city, we will be able to speed up that day when all of God's children, black men and white men, Jews and Gentiles, Protestants and Catholics, will be able to join hands and sing in the words of the old Negro spiritual, "Free at last! Free at last! Thank God almighty, we are free at last!"

Public acclaim now made King a world figure, but he saw his real work taking place in marches, churches, jails, and streets throughout America. First in Montgomery, he had walked and preached to support a boycott of public buses. It fit right in with the social-action ministry King and Dexter Baptist had begun already. The bus boycott and the rallies to support it proved immensely successful. When white officials in Montgomery tried to subvert the movement, King and other leaders arranged symbolic events and a volunteer carpool to keep up morale. When King was arrested first in January 1956 on spurious traffic charges and then in February on charges that he led in hindering operation of a

business "without just cause," his imprisonment and fines made national news. When his home was bombed, King took the occasion to
speak eloquently of Jesus' command to "love your enemies." He likewise used lessons from the Indian leader Mohandas K. Gandhi, whose
writings King read voraciously.

As the Montgomery boycott, appeals of King's conviction, and
white violent activity in various parts of the country continued, King
grew increasingly dependent on a militant nonviolent approach to civil
rights. He said the tactics came from Gandhi and the spirit came from
Jesus. At last, in November 1956, the U.S. Supreme Court struck down
Alabama's segregation laws concerning public transportation. King and
other ministers boarded buses on 21 December 1956 as legal integration
began in that city. Churches and political events focused on the preaching
and teaching of Dr. King.

By this time King's efforts had begun to receive the attention of a
broader audience, but publication of his book *Stride Toward Freedom*
and an official visit to Ghana to celebrate independence for that new
nation did not distract him from his work among the poor and the oppressed. Arrested and beaten in Montgomery in September, King chose
to serve a term in jail rather than pay a fine, in protest of the injustice of
the justice system, but the commissioner of the court paid his fine and he
was released.

Early in 1960, King moved with his family to Atlanta, where he stayed
in close touch with many of the local efforts across the South to end
segregation. Student groups in Greensboro, Nashville, and elsewhere
had started sit-ins at segregated lunch counters and department stores.
King helped them organize the Student Non-Violent Coordinating Committee, served on the Committee's adult advisory board, and helped raise
money for the organization as well as for the SCLC. He helped the
Freedom Riders, a group organized by the Congress of Racial Equality
when white hoodlums attacked them in Anniston and Montgomery, Alabama. The white mobs almost destroyed the church of Ralph Abernathy
that night, but federal marshals fought them off in what came to be called
"the Battle of Montgomery."

King answered what he termed a "Macedonian call" from Albany,
Georgia, and throughout most of 1962 he labored with the people there.
New, kinder tactics from the city administration and factionalism among
local civil rights leaders aided in foiling attempts to desegregate the city's
public areas. King was jailed on several occasions, and he had to deal
with the broken promises of white leaders and accusations from many
that he was a "communist" and a "dishonest agitator."

The movement coalesced again around severe, racist conditions in Birmingham in early 1963. Dr. King was once more arrested and jailed, and this time he was placed in solitary confinement. He responded to white clergy critics with his "Letter from Birmingham Jail," published widely throughout the world. He explained that he had come to Birmingham "because injustice exists here." He compared his own bearing of "the gospel of freedom" to that of Paul and the prophets of the eighth century B.C. He spoke of the larger issues involved in his struggle: "Injustice anywhere is a threat to justice everywhere." He wrote of the timeliness of the movement, the need for white moderate commitment, and of the morality of civil rights in a "higher law" context. He contrasted the weakness of the church in contemporary society with its strength during New Testament times.

> The judgment of God is upon the church as never before. If today's church does not recapture the sacrificial spirit of the early church, it will lose its authenticity, forfeit the loyalty of millions, and be dismissed as an irrelevant social club with no meaning for the 20th century. Every day I meet young people whose disappointment with the church has turned into outright disgust.

The release of King did not bring an end to the Birmingham crusade. Thousands of blacks, adults and children, confronted fire hoses, fierce police dogs, bombings, and beatings. By the end of May the nonviolent movement had resulted in enforced desegregation of many locations in that city.

WASHINGTON, STOCKHOLM, AND WORLD CITIZENSHIP

King led the March on Washington in the summer of 1963. In January 1964 he was designated *Time* magazine's "Man of the Year," and in October of that year he received notice of having won the Nobel Peace Prize. But the international attention he received as a result of his efforts concerning American race relationships, did not make him complacent. He kept up the pressure in such places as St. Augustine, Florida, where whites were particularly vicious and threatening. They had beaten Andrew Young, a young SCLC leader, and kicked him as he lay unconscious. Many demonstrators had been attacked, and King naturally intervened in person. Local leaders claimed that King was a "communist," creating turmoil in America to serve Russian interests. As usual,

King was arrested (despite the fact that a judge had permitted demonstrations). Even in such a context SCLC was able to opened the way for biracial negotiations and an end to much of the public segregation that had been a way of life.

King was present when President Johnson signed the 1964 Civil Rights Bill into law in July. Later he was in New York helping cool down the situation after blacks in the ghettos of Newark and Harlem rioted. He was in Mississippi in late July to help publicize a Freedom Summer campaign. Campaigns for equal education, voter registration drives, and other efforts involved thousands of whites and blacks from throughout the nation. King went to Vicksburg, Meridian, and Philadelphia (where three young workers had just disappeared). In August, he spoke at the Democratic Party convention in New Jersey, asking for a new bill of rights for the disadvantaged.

In early 1965, King met another test of the newly guaranteed civil rights when he joined the SCLC, SNCC, and other organizations that were seeking to register blacks to vote in Selma, Alabama. A racist sheriff, Jim Clark, who wore a button inscribed "Never," led the opposition. Hundreds marched, picketed, and demonstrated in behalf of their rights. King was arrested, but he managed to lead the movement from his cell. An immense march to the state capitol drew civil rights advocates from across the nation—as well as Ku Klux Klan, American Nazi, and White Citizen Council adversaries. Violence kept erupting. Eventually President Johnson felt constrained to lobby in behalf of a comprehensive Voting Rights Bill, which sailed through congress.

A TIME FOR DECISION

As King was drawn into the strife in Boston, Los Angeles, New York, Detroit, and elsewhere during what was called "the long hot summer" of 1965, his concern over American involvement in Vietnam was increasing. By himself, with trusted advisors, and outside experts, he began to study the nature of the conflict, the disproportionate black participation as soldiers were sent, and the relationship of civil rights to international citizenship.

Already hounded by J. Edgar Hoover and accused of being a communist, King knew the accusations that he was a subversive would increase if he criticized the growing war effort. Columnist Max Freedman chided, "Is he casting about for a role in Vietnam because the civil rights struggle is no longer adequate to his own estimate of his talents?"

But to be consistent with his stance throughout his career, did he not have to confront injustice wherever he discovered it? Either he would have to speak out against the war, or by silence he would indicate his agreement with the administration, which claimed a "great concensus" in behalf of support for the government of South Vietnam. King pondered his alternatives, and he tried to anticipate the consequences of various actions.

SELECTED BIBLIOGRAPHY

Ansbro, John J. *Martin Luther King: The Making of a Mind.* Maryknoll, N.Y.: Orbis Books, 1982.

Bennett, Lerone, Jr. *What Manner of Man? Martin Luther King, Jr.* Chicago: Johnson Publishing, 1964.

Fager, Charles E. "Dilemma for Dr. King." *Christian Century,* 16 March 1966, pp. 331-32.

King, Martin Luther, Jr. "Letter from Birmingham Jail." *Christian Century,* 12 June 1963, pp. 767-73.

_____. *Stride Toward Freedom: The Montgomery Story.* New York: Harper & Row, 1958.

_____. *The Trumpet of Conscience.* New York: Harper & Row, 1967.

_____. *Where Do We Go From Here: Chaos or Community.* New York: Harper & Row, 1967.

Lewis, David L. *King: A Critical Biography.* New York: Praeger, 1970.

Lincoln, C. Eric, ed. *Martin Luther King, Jr.: A Profile.* New York: Hill & Wang, 1970.

Oates, Stephen. *Let the Trumpet Sound: The Life of Martin Luther King, Jr.* San Francisco: Harper & Row, 1982.

Billy Graham and Worldwide Evangelization

This case was prepared by Garth M. Rosell

Billy Graham felt a deep sense of gratitude to God as he gazed out over the nearly four thousand participants gathered at the RAI Center in Amsterdam that warm July evening in 1983. What had started as only a dream in the late 1950s had now become a reality. Women and men from 132 nations of the world—the majority of whom had never before attended a conference of any kind and nearly seventy percent of whom had come from Third World countries—had joined together to form the first International Conference of Itinerant Evangelists.

In a career marked by many achievements and honors, it is quite possible that this gathering was for Billy Graham the most joyous and satisfying of them all. Certainly its basic themes lay at the very center of that ministry to which he felt God had called him many years before. "While the social needs of man call for our urgent attention," Graham told his assembled colleagues in the closing address of the conference, "We believe that ultimately these needs can be met only in and through the gospel. Humankind's basic need is to be born from above—to be converted to Christ." Their task together, he told them, was nothing less than worldwide evangelization.

Who could have imagined, in those early years, that the first son born to Frank and Morrow Graham 7 November 1918 would grow up to become one of the major religious figures of the twentieth century? On the contrary, the lanky boy who helped out on the family's three-hundred-acre dairy farm near Charlotte, North Carolina, and who sat with his brother Melvin, his sisters Catherine and Jean, and his parents in the little congregation of the Associate Reformed Presbyterian Church (General Synod) which the family attended some five miles from their home, did not seem especially destined for prominence. Indeed, it was not until his religious conversion in 1934, under the preaching of a southern evangelist named Mordecai Fowler Ham, that Billy Frank's interests seemed to turn in new directions. Following a summer of work as Fuller Brush salesmen, Billy and his good friend Grady Wilson entered Bob Jones College in the fall of 1936. After a semester, he transferred to the Florida Bible Institute near Tampa, where, prompted by Dean John Minder, he had his first taste of preaching. It was there, in March of 1938, that on his knees under the stars Billy felt God's call to ministry and promised God that if he wanted him to preach, he would do it. In 1939, he was ordained as a Southern Baptist minister by the St. John's Association at Peniel.

In 1940, Billy Graham enrolled at Wheaton College (Illinois), where he majored in anthropology, graduating three years later with a B.A. degree. While there he met Ruth Bell, the daughter of Presbyterian medical missionaries in China, and the two were married in August of 1943. Rather than go on to theological seminary, however, Billy accepted a call to the Village Church, a little Baptist church in Western Springs, a suburb of Chicago. On the recommendation of Torrey Johnson, a prominent pastor and professor in the Chicago area, the Village Church took over leadership of "Songs in the Night," a Sunday evening radio broadcast. Along with George Beverly Shea, who had agreed to join him for the broadcast, Billy went on the air with "Songs in the Night" in January of 1944. Through the efforts of Torrey Johnson, Billy Graham also became involved as the first evangelist for the newly organized Youth for Christ.

Although actively involved in preaching both in America and abroad during the next several years, it was not until the Los Angeles Crusade in 1949 that Billy gained national prominence. It was in that remarkable series of meetings held in a tent at Washington and Hill Streets in Los Angeles that Stuart Hamblen (the well-known songwriter), Jim Vaus (a twice-convicted wiretapper), and Louis Zamperini (an Olympic runner) responded to Graham's call for decision. The conversions of these well-known figures, combined with the famous directive of William Randolph Hearst to "puff Graham," helped to create a tremendous interest in the crusade. Under the ministry of the Graham team, several hundred "hit the sawdust trail" each night. Eight weeks of meetings finally came to an end on the twentieth of November with a crowd far larger than the nine thousand seats could hold.

The Los Angeles Crusade marked the beginning of what has now been nearly four decades of similar gatherings in cities and towns around the world. Nearly one hundred million people have attended the Crusades and many more millions have been touched by Billy Graham's ministry through radio, television, books, and films. Graham's evangelistic outreach has been further facilitated through such organizations as the Billy

Graham Evangelistic Association (founded in 1950), "Hour of Decision" radio broadcasts (started in 1950), *Christianity Today* (started in 1956), *Decision* magazine (founded in 1960), and the Billy Graham Center (dedicated in 1980).

While unique in some respects, there can be little doubt that Billy Graham's ministry is a more contemporary reflection of the much older revival tradition in American religious history. The great eras of spiritual awakening—most notably, the Great Awakening of the 1720s and 1730s (led by individuals such as Theodore Frelinghuysen, Gilbert Tennent, Jonathan Edwards, and George Whitefield), the Second Great Awakening of the early nineteenth century (led by individuals such as Asahel Nettleton, Timothy Dwight, and Charles G. Finney), the later nineteenth- and early twentieth-century awakenings (guided by figures such as Dwight L. Moody and Billy Sunday), and the mid-twentieth century awakenings (pioneered by preachers such as Torrey Johnson and Mervin Rosell)—helped to bring new life and vitality to America's churches. United by a common authority (the Bible), a common experience (conversion), and a common vision (worldwide evangelization), revivalists such as Billy Graham have throughout the centuries of the church's history attempted to call sinners to repentance, the faithful to obedience to the biblical mandates, and the whole church to worldwide evangelization.

It is this worldwide vision, marked by Graham's own travels to such places as Australia and Russia, that seems to have given focus during the late 1950s to the idea of bringing together itinerant evangelists from every part of the world. Never before in the history of the Christian church had such a conference been held. It was not until the 1980s, however, that Graham's dream was to become a reality.

Under the auspices of the Billy Graham Evangelistic Association, Walter Smyth was selected as chairman, Werner Burklin was named as director, and Leighton Ford was appointed program chairman of what was to be called an International Conference of Itinerant Evangelists. Amsterdam was selected as the site for the gathering because it combined good facilities and a good communications network with easy access of travel visas. After months of planning and hard work by the international staff, the nearly four thousand participants arrived representing 132 countries from around the world.

From the opening flag ceremony to the closing communion service, it was clear that this was no ordinary conference. Rather, it was a coming together of practitioners from virtually every race and culture, holding the promise of the kind of worldwide evangelization that had remained the very center of Billy Graham's own life and ministry. The fifteen Amsterdam Affirmations that were overwhelmingly endorsed by the conference delegates form a kind of manifesto for worldwide evangelization in the coming decades. With only limited years remaining in his own ministry, Billy Graham could only gaze out across that vast multitude of colleagues and give thanks to God that they would be carrying on this strategic task.

SELECTED BIBLIOGRAPHY

Graham, Billy. *A Biblical Standard for Evangelists: A Commentary on the Fifteen Affirmations Made by Participants at the International Conference for Itinerant Evangelists in Amsterdam, the Netherlands, July 1983.* Minneapolis: World Wide Publications, 1984.

High, Stanley. *Billy Graham.* New York: McGraw-Hill, 1956.

McLoughlin, William G., Jr. *Billy Graham: Revivalist in a Secular Age.* New York: Ronald Press, 1960.

_____. *Modern Revivalism: Charles Grandison Finney to Billy Graham.* New York: Ronald Press, 1959.

Pollock, John. *Billy Graham: Evangelist to the World.* San Francisco: Harper & Row, 1979.

_____. *To All the Nations: The Billy Graham Story.* San Francisco: Harper & Row, 1985.

Exhibit 1

Amsterdam Affirmations

Affirmation I: We confess Jesus Christ as God, our Lord and Savior, who is revealed in the Bible, which is the infallible Word of God.

Affirmation II: We affirm our commitment to the Great Commission of our Lord, and we declare our willingness to go anywhere, do anything, and sacrifice anything God requires of us in the fulfillment of that Commission.

Affirmation III: We respond to God's call to the biblical ministry of the evangelist, and accept our solemn responsibility to preach the Word to all peoples as God gives opportunity.

Affirmation IV: God loves every human being, who, apart from faith in Christ, is under God's judgment and destined for hell.

Affirmation V: The heart of the biblical message is the good news of God's salvation, which comes by grace alone through faith in the risen Lord Jesus Christ and his atoning death on the cross for our sins.

Affirmation VI: In our proclamation of the Gospel we recognize the urgency of calling all to decision to follow Jesus Christ as Lord and Savior, and to do so lovingly and without coercion or manipulation.

Affirmation VII: We need and desire to be filled and controlled by the Holy Spirit as we bear witness to the Gospel of Jesus Christ, because God alone can turn sinners from their sin and bring them to everlasting life.

Affirmation VIII: We acknowledge our obligation, as servants of God, to lead lives of holiness and moral purity, knowing that we exemplify Christ to the church and to the world.

Affirmation IX: A life of regular and faithful prayer and Bible study is essential to our personal spiritual growth, and to our power for ministry.

Affirmation X: We will be faithful stewards of all that God gives us, and will be accountable to others in the finances of our ministry, and honest in reporting our statistics.

Affirmation XI: Our families are a responsibility given to us by God, and are a sacred trust to be kept as faithfully as our call to minister to others.

Affirmation XII: We are responsible to the church, and will endeavor always to conduct our ministries so as to build up the local body of believers and serve the church at large.

Affirmation XIII: We are responsible to arrange for the spiritual care of those who come to faith under our ministry, to encourage them to identify with the local body of believers, and seek to provide for the instruction of believers in witnessing to the Gospel.

Affirmation XIV: We share Christ's deep concern for the personal and social sufferings of humanity, and we accept our responsibility as Christians and as evangelists to do our utmost to alleviate human need.

Affirmation XV.   We beseech the body of Christ to join with us in prayer and work for peace in our world, for revival and a renewed dedication to the biblical priority of evangelism in the church, and for the oneness of believers in Christ for the fulfillment of the Great Commission, until Christ returns.

Index

185